Hidden Voices

Reflections of a Gay, Catholic Priest

Gary M. Meier

STATEMENT OF CONFIDENTIALITY

Throughout this book, names and details have been changed to protect the identities of those involved. All the stories are true.

www.fathergary.com

TABLE OF CONTENTS

Forward to the Second Edition

The first edition of "Hidden Voices, Reflections of a Gay Catholic Priest" was published anonymously in 2011.

Today, the second edition is now published with one difference – it is no longer anonymous. It is being published under the name of its author, me – Gary M. Meier.

The decision to publish "Hidden Voices" anonymously allowed me the freedom to say what I wanted to say publicly and continue ministering as a Catholic Priest. In other words, as long as I remained anonymous, I could remain in ministry doing what I was called to do and being who I was called to be. At the same time, I always knew there might come a time when being anonymous would no longer be enough. Now is that time.

***

A lot has happened since the first edition was published. Six months after I sold my first copy, I began a leave of absence from the priesthood. In some ways, I had been preparing to take a leave of absence for years. I have tried over the years to reconcile my silence as a gay priest with that of the Church's increasingly antigay stance. I have been unsuccessful. Because I have met several times with my bishop in recent years to discuss my struggle, it was no surprise to him when I requested a leave of absence for the purpose of discerning my relationship in the church.

He graciously expressed some sadness on behalf of the people I serve and affirmed my autonomy to choose what was best for me. I decided to tell my parishioners that I would be taking a leave of absence to do two things; first, go to graduate school to pursue a Master's Degree in counseling, which I am currently doing; and second, to discern what ministry God is calling me to. I was proud of the wording, 'to discern what ministry God was calling me to.' It is a true statement, true enough that it has integrity and at the same time it was not the complete truth. And, while I have no proof of this, I think my parishioners knew there was more to the story – but they were graciously willing to support me and give me the space I was seeking without asking too many questions.

So, six months after the first edition of hidden voices was published, I began a leave of absence – a leave of absence which was long overdue, and the right thing to do. I have never doubted, nor do I doubt my call to the priesthood. I have no doubt that God called me to the priesthood and at the same time, I have no doubt that God has called me to my current status. While this may seem contradictory at first, I don't believe it is. At the heart of every authentic calling is the desire to live a life of integrity. It was my desire to live a life of integrity that led me to the priesthood and it is that same desire that has led me to where I am today. Initially, I was hopeful that I could figure out a way to have integrity while remaining part of a hierarchy that is antigay – I was unsuccessful. It was July, 2012 and the presidential election campaign was in full swing, and so was the hierarchy. At least once or twice a week, some member of the hierarchy would issue an antigay statement in an effort to persuade the Catholic vote. Some bishops even went as far as to threaten the 'salvation' of anyone who supported a candidate who didn't believe as the church did. In the end it became clear that I could not be both gay and a priest – that is, I could not live as a gay priest which means living in silence while publicly pretending to support the hierarchy's teachings on homosexuality.

So, the second edition of "Hidden Voices, Reflections of a Gay Catholic Priest" by Gary M. Meier was published. I am not sure where exactly any of this will lead. It is a huge leap of faith and to be perfectly honest with you, very frightening. I know that while many will celebrate and be grateful for this publication, others will be angry and upset and feel as if I am betraying the church. I have no such intention, I am just a man trying to live a life of integrity and speak the truth that God has given me to speak. I do not mean the church any harm and in fact I still love the church very much. In fact, I see my speaking out as an act of love toward a community which was born of God's radical inclusivity. Somehow we have lost that, particularly toward the LGBT community. I would like to see us get it back.

Thank you and God Bless,

Gary M. Meier

Chapter One

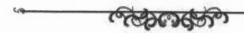

Silent and Shamed

I am a gay, Catholic priest. I may very well be *your* parish priest, right now presiding at the mass at the church up the road. And I am not alone. Like so many of my brothers and sisters called to the ministry, I believe the Church's teaching on homosexuality has caused and continues to cause harm to many gay men and women, young and old, who are looking for acceptance and love but instead find silence and shame. I recently had a meeting with my Bishop to discuss this struggle.

As the conversation began, I found myself positively accepted as a gay priest; I found my ministry continually affirmed. As far as Bishop meetings go – this one was turning out to be a pretty good one. At one point in the conversation, however, I realized that he didn't quite understand my struggle. My struggle isn't with being gay. I know I'm gay. I knew I was gay the day I went into the seminary, and I have long come to accept my orientation as a part of who I am, celebrating it as a gift from God and not a cross to bear. I didn't choose the priesthood and celibacy as a way to avoid my orientation; I choose them, like so many other priests, because God had called me to them. I tried to clarify:

"My struggle isn't with being gay, it's with the Church's teaching on homosexuality and the way in which the hierarchy is interpreting that teaching regarding the homosexual person, the ordination of gay men, gay marriage, gay parenting, and especially the impact that this teaching has on gay youth growing up in the Church. This is what I struggle with."

"We don't have to lead with that teaching, you know."

"Good answer. But so many bishops and priest *are* leading with that teaching." I leaned in slightly and looked him directly in the eye. "A bishop once tried to explain 'intrinsically disordered' to 1,500 youth from this diocese at a youth rally by comparing homosexuality to alcoholism. I once witnessed another bishop tell a group of nearly 500 youth leaving for the prolife march in Washington D.C., that 'gay marriage is one of the most serious prolife issues we face today because it's a threat to the sanctity of marriage.' Do you realize just how damaging that can be to those young people who are struggling with their orientation? It's hard enough to be a 'straight' teenager dealing with the standard ups and downs of hormones and emotions, but to be a teenager with same sex attractions in a community where your spiritual leaders, the people you look to for guidance and affirmation, are telling you that you have a disease like alcoholism and that you're a threat to life—can anyone survive it intact? Yet that's precisely the message our Church is sharing. LGBT youth are hearing that they are disordered, diseased, defective, damaged goods, wrong when they should be right. Do you have any idea just how destructive that can be to someone who is struggling, confused and scared? To someone who prays every night that this 'thing,' these attractions, would just go away? That he or she could just be good? It's no surprise that so many teenage suicides are attributed to orientation issues. Can we deny that we, as the Church, are part of those struggles, those deaths, that we, as the Church, are creating an environment that pushes kids into silence and shame? That's my struggle, Bishop – when our Church leaders 'lead' with those teaching, it causes a tremendous amount of harm, creating a culture of silence and shame that is immeasurably damaging to our youth."

"But not every bishop leads with that teaching, let me assure you."

"Thank God," I said. "But too many do and it only takes

one, one priest's snide pulpit remarks, one bishop's tacit denunciation. I can tell you for certain that when you're a teenager, and you think you may be gay but you're not sure – anytime you hear the word gay or homosexual or queer, you tune in. You can be in a room full of people, engaged with friends when someone across the rooms says the word gay and still, you'll hear every word. You can be doing your homework in the next room, when the word homosexual blares from the TV, and you'll automatically tune in to what's being said. You can pass by a book store and see dozens of books being advertised, but you'll only see the one with the word queer in its title. You tune into every conversation overheard in passing, every word spoken, every book written that has to do with homosexuality – because they're talking about *you* – and you want to know what they're saying. I'm glad not every bishop or priest leads with that teaching, but it only takes one priest's 'leading' to cause serious harm."

***

And they do. Since the pedophilia scandals of 2002, more and more bishops *are* 'leading' with that teaching in one way or another. Recently, in Denver, Colorado the diocese refused to re-enroll two children in Catholic school because their parents are lesbians.[i] In Minnesota, the bishop recently mailed nearly 400,000 DVD's to oppose same-sex partnerships, stating that same-sex unions potentially weaken society's already damaged foundation.[ii] Archbishop Timothy Dolan from New York City recently told CNN in response to the passing of a gay marriage law in New York, that "I was sad. I'm just sad because I think it's [gay marriage] not good for the common good."[iii] During Gay Pride weekend, a priest in Boston was asked to cancel his "All Are Welcomed" mass because it supported the 'gay agenda.' Unbelievable! In part of his homily, this Boston priest questioned this hierarchal mandate: "Some people have said that by celebrating a liturgy we were supporting a Gay Pride agenda. I confess I don't know what that is. As a Catholic, my only agenda — just like Jesus — is to love and accept one another." [iv] I can only wonder how the hierarchy would treat Jesus if he were around today and invited the sinners and marginalized, tax collectors and prostitutes, gays and lesbians, to dinner.

Am I the only one who thinks the teachings of the Church and the way they're being interpreted by our hierarchy is harmful? How does being in a loving committed relationship weaken society? How does gay marriage oppose the common good? Why would we intentionally cause emotional stress and harm to children by removing them from Catholic schools? Why on earth would we cancel an "All Are Welcomed" mass? Are we crazy?

***

The 8th Day Center for Justice, a Catholic organization staffed by 30 congregations of nuns, priests, and brothers dedicated to analysis and action related to the promotion of "justice, equality and human dignity among all people regardless of race, ethnicity, religion, abilities, gender, sexual orientation, or socio-economic class" recently issued a statement saying that "the teachings of the Church and the behavior of some members of the Church hierarchy have added to an atmosphere of bullying and intimidation."[v] They go on to say that "despite claims to the contrary... people of differing sexual orientation are not welcome in the Church. Moreover, such discrimination contributes to an atmosphere in society which promotes bigotry and violence toward the LGBT community."[vi] Bullying, intimidation, discrimination, bigotry and violence—is this what our Church is about? Do we want to create an atmosphere of silence and shame? The current climate in our Church doesn't foster a safe place for those who are trying to 'figure it out.' Instead, we're driving people away.

This book is for all of those who are being or have been driven away. And that's not just the gay population; it's all of those who have accepted a member of their family, all of those who have allied as friends. They too have been silenced and shamed, ostracized by a Church teaching and hierarchal positioning that will not allow us to support, love, nurture and foster positive gay relationships in our Church.

A friend of mine recently sent me a mobile picture of his parents who attended a Gay Pride celebration with their lesbian daughter. I remember seeing the picture and thinking to myself how awesome it was that his parents were able to support their daughter even though their Church wouldn't. As a Catholic school teacher, Mom could lose her job if this picture got into the wrong hands–more silence, more shame. I've known this family for years, your typical Catholic suburban family with six children, one of whom is a lesbian. They have always been strong supporters of their Catholic faith and are very active members at their parish. It saddens me to think and humbles me to realize that they continue to support a Church that will not support them. Couldn't it be another way? The slogan 'loud and proud' is often used in the gay community in an effort to counteract the oppression of others including the oppression of the Church. Might we as a Church come to support that culture, the culture of loud and proud over silence and shame?

***

I know I'm not the only one who believes it's time for a change. But as a member of the clergy, I also know I'm not allowed to publically oppose these teachings, unless I'm ready to leave active ministry. It's an ongoing struggle of integrity for me—do I speak the truth in an age when the truth so desperately needs to be spoken, or do I remain hidden, practicing the ministry that God has called me towards as a Catholic priest? It's a choice none of us should have to make, a choice I daily have to make, a choice thousands of priests daily have to make.

So, why write this book? To give voice to the hidden, to those thousands of voices that feel the way I do and to give hope, albeit just a little, to those who struggle with the Church's stance on homosexuality. By writing, I begin to negotiate this struggle of integrity, I begin to give voice to the truth that I know along with so many other struggling gay Catholics, gay priests. The Church's teachings and the way it's being communicated by some of our bishops is disgraceful, harmful and even lethal. What follows are some of my reflections on what it means to negotiate life as a gay priest in the Catholic Church, to struggle with self and hierarchy, and to move from silence and shame to hope and forgiveness. Thank you for your support.

Chapter Two

I Want to be Out

I have been struggling with the Church's hierarchy and teachings since 2002, the year the sexual abuse scandal in America broke and the Church began actively scapegoating homosexuals for the pedophilia crisis. For those of us who are gay priests, this attack is both offensive and appalling. In 2005, the Church issued a document entitled "Instruction Concerning the Criteria for the Discernment of Vocations with regard to Persons with Homosexual Tendencies in view of their Admission to the Seminary and to Holy Orders;" [vii] The document states that it will no longer ordain gay men to the priesthood. Problem solved.

As if. Banning gay priests won't solve the pedophilia crisis, and every rational human being knows it, has known it for years. There have always been a very small percentage of people who have suffered from pedophilia, preying on innocent children, but there is no correlation to be found between this illness and a homosexual identity; even a 2011 John Jay Report drafted for the U.S. Conference of Catholic Bishops confirms this.[viii] In fact, the vast majority of pedophiles identify as heterosexual men and prey upon young family members—nieces, nephews, children, etc. They are not gay priests.[ix]

***

As we have all read in the news by now, the 2002 crisis in the Church was created, not by homosexuality, but by hierarchical neglect. When a priest was accused or caught sexually abusing a child, his superior would simply reassign him to a new parish, creating a situation where the abuse could occur again and again. The hierarchy, as we have now discovered, would rather reassign a pedophile priest a second and even third time, rather than admit it was wrong in reassigning him in the first place. Caught in a web of deceit and lies, the cover-ups deepened. It is appalling to learn that the Church knew as much as it did and never took the actions necessary to protect its children.

***

When the scandal broke in 2002, we were all shocked by the amount of abuse which had been occurring for years. How could so many priests be accused of doing so much harm which went against the very nature of what we as priests were called to do? Case after case was being exposed all over the media. For those of us who lived through that – it was awful. You never knew who was next. I can remember being on vacation with another priest and getting a phone call telling me about three more priests who had been removed from ministry. These were guys we knew. I can remember hanging up the phone and telling my priest friend that 'three more fell today.' It was an interesting choice of words – fell. They had fallen hard. And the Church was falling fast. It was an awful time to be a priest.

I can remember debating time and time again whether or not I should wear my Roman collar in public. When I did, I knew I would get stares and glares from people as I passed by. Everyone who wore a collar was suspect. I can remember one man coming up to me on the street, pointing at me with anger and sadness in his eyes as he said, "I will never trust my children with you." The only response I could give was, "Don't let your children around anyone you don't trust." I felt sick–"This is not what I signed up for!" It was an awful situation, and it was just beginning.

***

One morning, around 8:00 A.M., there was a knock on the door of the rectory where I was assigned as an associate priest. When I answered, there were eight men and women dressed in three piece suits with police badges dangling from their necks. They asked for the pastor, who had come out of his office to see who was at the door. When I pointed at him, without asking, they came in and escorted him to his office. None of them said a word. In a few minutes, three of them came out and went upstairs to his room, still no word. Soon others arrived and they too were coming and going, in and out of the office, to his room, back and forth. I asked one of them to tell me what was going on, what was happening? It was all happening so fast; the staff were all wondering what was going on; questions were being asked with few answers forthcoming. Finally, the one in charge took me into another office and explained that my pastor was being placed under arrest for child pornography charges. What?! I was stunned, nervous and sickened. I was overwhelmed. What should I do? The rectory was situated in the heart of the parish campus, next to the school and Church, and I feared that a lot of people might find out, or worse, see their pastor being taken away in handcuffs. What should I do?

I asked if I could speak to the pastor and was given permission. I had so many mixed feelings—anger, fear, disgust, concern, worry. I can't remember everything we spoke about, but I do remember asking how he was doing and if there was someone I needed to call for him. He asked me to call the Archbishop and let him know what was happening. I also said to him, more as a question really, that "the police told me they were looking for child pornography." To which he replied, "Yes." I didn't have to ask him if they were going to find any.

By early afternoon, he was being escorted out of the rectory, without the handcuffs, and was taken away. Just like that. I spoke to the Archbishop once that day and he asked only two questions, "Did he admit to it?" and "How was he doing?" I can't remember the order in which he asked them. Unbelievably, we made it through that day without the media finding out. With the exception of the staff, no one knew, but not for long.

***

By 5:30 A.M. the next morning, the media was crowded out front of the church. Someone was knocking on the door of the rectory yet again. This time it was a parishioner who was concerned about the media presence and who, thankfully, wanted to know how I was doing. As of yet no information had been made public and no names had been released. I told the media they could be in the public space outside the church but that they were not allowed in the church or on church property.

By mid-morning, my phone was ringing off the hook. The media was reporting that one of the priests at my parish was under arrest for the possession of child pornography. There were only two of us assigned there, and people were calling me to find out which one of us was guilty. I can remember telling the Archbishop, who asked me not to do any interviews with the media, that either he or I had to make an announcement and soon. He agreed to do it through the media office for the diocese, and at noon, just in time for the news, the Communications Director held a press conference.

The days that followed are a blur. There were parish-wide meetings, school board meetings, parish council meetings, school parent meetings, prayer meetings, and others I can't remember. On the weekend, the Archbishop came and spoke at all the masses, with all the media present.

No one could believe this was happening. No one could believe our pastor had done what he had done. No one could believe this was hitting so close to home. We were all filled with disbelief, shock, anger, disgust, and compassion. It's so incredibly humbling and hard to watch a man's life crushed before your eyes. The fall from grace is not a pretty thing to see.

***

Could there have been something done to prevent this? Could the Church have done more to make sure its priests weren't isolated, weren't tempted to do what they were eventually caught doing? Absolutely. There is much to be done and much that can be done to make the Church a better Church, to make the priesthood a better priesthood. But it has to begin with a willingness to admit that there are things that we've done *wrong*. "You'll never fix the problem if you can't admit the problem" a professor of mine used to say. An attitude of denial is the enemy of change.

Yet that is precisely the attitude our Church has today adopted. The hierarchy won't admit the problem. *We* won't admit the problem. And the problem is *not* gay priests.

According to *America Magazine*, it is estimated that anywhere from 23% to 58% of the priest in the Catholic

Church are gay.[x] That's a staggering statistic. While there's no way to verify those numbers, given that the voices of gay priests remain hidden, suffice to say, if only the most conservative end of this estimated range is true, it remains proof enough that gay priests are not the problem anymore than straight priests are.[xi] If they were, the scale of the crisis would be so much greater.

My own experiences confirm this. Unlike pedophile priests, the majority of the gay priests that I know have healthy sexual identities. They believe their homosexuality is a gift from God. They recognize that this is how they were created, and they are not ashamed. They have embraced it as part of who they are. They are in the process of living a life of integration, love, and are compassionate people who are doing incredible work in their ministry to bring others closer to God through the sacraments and the Church. Far from abusing children, these are the priests who welcome gay and straight couples alike into the Church, blessing their love, their unions. Like their straight counterparts, these priests live lives of celibate integrity. Scapegoating these men makes no sense given the realities of their lives; they are not to blame.

***

If gay priest aren't the problem, as the hierarchy suggests, who or what is? Ask most people in the pews if they're mad about the scandal of 2002 and they will say yes. Ask them who they're mad at, and you might be surprised. It's been my experience that the people in the pews, the Church, the body of Christ, are mad, not at gay priests, but at the Church hierarchy itself, for spending years covering up pedophilia in the Church, for systematically reassigning pedophile priests to other parishes only to have them offend again and again. Hundreds of victims could have been spared if the hierarchy would have made more responsible decisions. The bottom line is that the hierarchy has lost its credibility. We must stop denying this fact—the problem lies in the hierarchy itself, its approach to the scandal and its response in the years since.

***

The success of Dan Brown's *Da Vinci Code* surprised the Church. Everyone was reading it. I was getting so many questions about it that I had to read it myself so that I would know how best to answer them. The reason it became so popular, I believe, was that the book centers on a hierarchal cover up, a cover up wholly un-related to pedophilia but a cover up none-the-less. People were already asking questions of the Church. If the hierarchy was covering up pedophilia, maybe they've been covering up something else as well? The timing of the book's release was accidental, but extremely beneficial. As sales numbers suggest, the hierarchy *has* lost the respect of the people. It can no longer be trusted.

That's the real problem we face as a Church, a problem brought to light by the scandal of 2002: we have a leadership that we cannot trust to address issues head-on. When the hierarchy speaks, the people cautiously listen, but they're not afraid to question that authority anymore – and the hierarchy doesn't deal well with questions.

***

This tension today between the hierarchy and the people can be a remarkably constructive thing if we stop denying the problems that we, as a Church, face. It might even be the catalyst we need to allow the Church to develop and grow. But we're not there yet. Denial continues as the hierarchy repeatedly asserts its moral authority through encyclicals and proclamations, while refusing to hear the hidden voices of not only gay

Catholics, but divorced Catholics, separated Catholics, single parent Catholics and others.

Though the people aren't listening like they use to, the hierarchy keeps trying. In fact, on every civil rights issue pertaining to homosexuality the Catholic Church has come out with statements against the fundamental rights of gays. Not only in our country, but around the world. I was appalled to read that the Vatican had issued a statement against the U.N.'s decision to boycott certain countries that criminalize and punish homosexuals in their country.[xii] I was appalled to read that the United States Conference of Catholic Bishop's had issued a statement opposing a non-discrimination bill in our country.[xiii] And I continue to be appalled by the absurdity of refusing the ordination of gay men to the priesthood that's been in effect since 2005.

***

Does our Church really need to be this way? What do we have to fear? I recently attended my first Pride Fest, and if I had to sum up my experience in two words they would be: loud and proud. It was an amazing experience to witness, tens of thousands of gays and lesbians and their supporters being precisely that. Having lived for so long in a hierarchical atmosphere of silence and shame, it was liberating to be loud and proud – albeit only for a moment and in another city to avoid being recognized.

There has always been a part of me that has wanted to attend a Pride Fest, but to be honest; there's also been a part of me that hasn't. Before attending, like so many others, my only impression of Pride Fest had been from reports on the news. These reports always seemed to depict the pride parade in a way that seemed weird, crazy and far out. Images of cross dressers, dykes, transvestites, and men wearing hardly anything fill the airwaves in a thirty second television blast. Pride has always been portrayed as something radical and controversial, something best to avoid, particularly given my identity as a Catholic priest. After all, as the 2005 document maintains, we're not allowed to "promote the gay agenda." While it could certainly be argued that merely attending a Pride Fest is not supporting the gay agenda per say, a news clip of a Catholic priest watching the parade go by (and cheering) would be controversial to say the least. To avoid the controversy and to remain a priest, I had never attended a Pride Fest, until now. This year was different; this year I wanted to see for myself, and in some small way, participate in the movement. With that goal in mind, a friend of mine and I attended Gay Pride in New York City.

***

The day before the main event, my friend and I were walking down 6th Avenue when we noticed what appeared to be a parade of some sort, so we decided to investigate. When we got close enough to see what was happening, we discovered it was a "Dyke Parade." There were thousands of lesbian women marching down the streets of New York chanting and celebrating. There were also lots of supporters lining the streets passing out literature. I stopped one of them to ask if she knew when the main Pride parade was going to be and where. She briefly gave me the information and told me to enjoy myself. And then I said, "I will, but I'm a little bit nervous, I've never been to a Pride Fest before."

"Oh, my gosh," she said, "You'll love it. *It's such a celebration of diversity and unity.* There's nothing to be nervous about, just enjoy it."

 Her enthusiastic description of Pride Fest as a celebration of diversity and unity really struck me. I couldn't help but think that when we as a Church are at our best, we too are a celebration of diversity in unity. When we as a Church are living the Gospel message, *we* celebrate diversity and unity. Her description of Pride Fest echoes so much of what the apostle Paul writes about in the scriptures, that "We are all one body, though we have many parts."[xiv] Shouldn't we describe the Church in the same way? As a celebration of diversity and unity?

***

The next day at the parade, I was surprised and pleased to see that the overwhelming majority of those attending the event were 'normal.' Having nothing but the images from the news media to go off of, my assumption and fear was that I would stand out, that everyone would be radically dressed or wearing nothing at all. That was not the reality. Don't get me wrong, there were plenty of wild and crazy outfits, but the overwhelming majority of those in attendance and in the parade were 'normal.' They were ordinary people belonging to ordinary groups like the firefighters, police, lawyers, volleyball teams, religious organizations, etc.; almost every conceivable group was represented. They're the person next door. They're the person you pass on the street every day. I can remember an overwhelming feeling of normalization as the day went by. It was liberating and refreshing to be in an environment that treats homosexuality not as a disorder but as normal, healthy and even sacred. It was indeed a celebration of unity and diversity, and for me personally, it was very freeing to move from an environment of silence and shame to loud and proud – if only for a day.

***

Since 2002, I have often thought about leaving active ministry because I'm not sure how much longer I can work for an organization which is so opposed to homosexuality, which actively supports the effort to discriminate and oppress gay people, which refuses to make room for the loud and proud. I have also thought about coming out publicly, going so far as to write a letter to that effect to release to the press. To paraphrase a scene from the movie "Milk," the late, great activist Harvey Milk says, "If every gay person came out, everyone would know at least one person who is gay and the discrimination would end."[xv] I think that way sometimes when it comes to the priesthood. I believe that if every gay priest would come out, the discrimination in our society and our Church would dramatically decrease.

**

"What is it you really want?" My priest friend asks, when I describe my struggle.

After a moment I reply, "I want to be out." My response caught me by surprise because the moment I said it, I knew it was true. I want to be out. It came with such clarity. I want the world to know the truth about who I am.

In the weeks that followed that conversation, I began to realize that what I really want is the truth to be out. I want the truth about homosexuality to be out. I want others to know that homosexuality is a gift. That you can live and love as God created you to love. We are created by love for love. Homosexuality is not a cross, it's not a curse, it's not an intrinsic disorder, *it is a gift*, created by love for love. It is a life-giving gift from God that embodies the infinite ways God's love can be manifested in our world. That's what I want. I want the truth to be out. I want people to know, to love and to respect one another by accepting this truth.

I am already out to family, friends, staff and many parishioners. It seems the older I get, the less I care about what other people think; I just want them to know me for who I am. I can remember when I decided to come out to my family; I did it because I wanted them to know me for who I am. I can remember telling one of my brothers that I thought it would be a shame if, at the end of my life, no one from the family knew one of the best things about me – so, I decided to share that part of my life with them. I can also remember coming out to some of my friends; they could barely believe it— "You're the straightest gay man I know!" There may come a time when I send my letter, when I come out more publicly and perhaps even from the pulpit, but until then, one thing is for certain, I feel compelled to support and live the truth that I have come to know through my relationship with God – the truth about love, the truth about homosexuality, the truth about being gay—and to share that truth with you.

Chapter Three

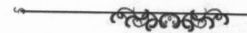

Conversion 1 & Conversion 2

What brought me here? How did I get to this point on my journey, the point where I'm ready to share the truth about who I am? In this chapter, I want to take a moment to tell my story, the story of how I came to be a gay, Catholic priest. I'm going to focus on two defining moments that I would call honest-to-God conversion experiences. The first conversion deals with acceptance of self and the second deals with acceptance of God. I would not be who I am today, I would not be able to share my story, without these sacred moments. To understand them in context, let's begin at the beginning.

***

I grew up in a typical, Catholic family household, a home where Church and family were the alpha and the omega, the institutions that defined our lives. Despite the dysfunctional, crazy drama of family life, complete with six children and an alcoholic father, every week we would don our Sunday bests and parade to Church, where my mother would do *her* best to keep us all quiet in the pews. That was no easy task. Lots of verbal and non-verbal reminders were shot down the pew to the kid that was making the most noise. It was not easy for mom, and it wasn't easy for us kids either. It felt like a prison; seven kids confined to a single row, mom on one side, dad on the other, with nothing to do, while all the while the background is filled with words that you never really heard or paid attention to. Needless to say, it was a breeding ground for giggling, nudging, tickling and shoving one another, all of which would send more looks straight down the pew. And when I say looks, I mean looks – there was the 'If you don't stop now – you're going to be sorry after mass' look or the 'Just wait till we get home' look. Then there was my personal favorite, the 'You better not let me catch you doing that again' look. From time to time, my mother would motion for one of us to come sit next to her, the dreaded 'Get over here right NOW look', beckoning us like the grim reaper herself. To ignore this look would be to sign our death sentence, so the switch would quickly be made.

Sitting next to mom was the worst place to sit. You couldn't do anything, and I mean anything. You had to sit like a statue, mumbling prayers. My brothers and I developed a game for getting into the pew at the beginning of mass, trying to position ourselves in the middle, as far away from mom or dad as possible. My older brothers were better at the game than I was and won more often than not, so needless to say, I spent a lot of masses in silence. The upside, I suppose, is that it allowed me to do a lot of day dreaming. And I did. I loved day dreaming, thinking about stuff, fantasizing about traveling, rescuing people, being a super hero, and on and on. There wasn't a children's liturgy of the word available to us at that time – at least if there was, we weren't allowed to go—so, hours were spent daydreaming. Church wasn't so bad really.

***

From the time we were little, family and Church came to us packaged with a certain set of values, including a particular understanding of homosexuality. We were never allowed to go into a public restroom alone; we always had to go with mom, well beyond what was considered age-appropriate. The reason? My mother feared one of us 'boys' would be abused in a public restroom. She would tell us that "dirty old men who like boys hang out there." Dirty old men. I didn't know it at the time, but that would shape my understanding of what it meant to be gay for years to come. Gays are nothing but dirty old men that hang out in restrooms and wait for little boys to come in. I'm sure you can see how that might traumatize a kid who was growing up with a lot of attractions he couldn't name or explain. I didn't know what being gay meant; I just knew I couldn't *be* gay because I wasn't a dirty old man.

***

I also remember the Phil Donahue show. I remember it so clearly because he would have on guests from time to time who were gay. It didn't seem to matter where in the house I was or what I was doing, if an advertisement came on about an upcoming show that would feature gays – I was all over it. I tuned in whenever it aired, though I wasn't even sure at the time why I was so interested. This show did let me know that there were different people out there, people who had different ways of living and thinking, but it also gave me more negative images of gay people. There were often features on struggling transsexual or transgendered individuals, episodes inevitably filled with yelling and screaming. On rare occasions, Phil would take a candid look at the struggle for acceptance of gay people and their families – more screaming, crying and hysteria. Whatever being gay was, I knew I didn't want to have anything to do with it. It was awful. It left an awful feeling in my gut.

***

Throughout grade school, I remember having very strong attractions towards my guy friends, but didn't everyone? One time, I spent the night at my friend's home. When it came time for bed, his undressing in front of me caused a very strong reaction, my first inklings of arousal. At the time I didn't know what that was, of course, other than a strong feeling, a heightened pulse and energy, an excitement.

A couple years later, I remember my brothers and I got a hold of an adult magazine. It featured mostly women, but there were a few pictures of men with the women. To this day, I couldn't tell you what the women were doing or how they looked in the pictures. But I can tell you exactly what the men were doing, where they were on the page, and what they looked like. I was absolutely drawn towards them, studying every inch of their bodies. Why?

In middle school, my best guy friend was 'dating' a girl whose best friend had a crush on me. This led to the four of us 'going out' from time to time, bike riding and stuff like that. When I think back to those days, I realize the only reason I went along was because I was attracted to my best friend and the best way to hang out with him was to pretend I liked his girlfriend's best friend. Looking at old pictures of the four of us now, I just smile and wonder if he knew. If *he* knew? I didn't even know! All I knew was I had a lot of energy towards my male friends, and that didn't seem so bad.

In high school, like so many teenagers, I started to sort myself out as a sexual being. I dated a girl my junior and senior year, and it was actually pretty cool. I was surprised by how much energy I had towards her. I can remember the sensation of 'floating' home the first time we kissed in front of her house. It was awesome! I wanted more of that feeling. The next time we made out in a park under a tree in front of a lake, I got a bit too "handsy." We didn't date too much after that. A few other girls came and went. While I had a definite attraction and energy towards them, it was never the same as the energy I had towards guys.

***

It's against this backdrop that I tried to figure out what was going on with me. By the time college came around, my head is filled with images of gay people who are dirty old men, transsexuals, people who create chaos everywhere they go. And yet, every chance I get to look at an adult magazine, I race through it looking for the guys. I know there is something different about me and my attractions but I can't possibly be gay—can I? My attractions were certainly different than my older brothers and my friends – but so what? What did they mean? What should I do with them?

Unsure of how to deal with those attractions, I decided to pursue an attraction that had slowly developed over my many years of pew-sitting, an attraction I *was* sure how to deal with—an attraction to the Church, to the priesthood. My freshmen year of college, I entered the seminary.

Oh my God, you would have thought my mother had died and gone to heaven. To have one of her sons interested in the priesthood – Oh My God! I would only last a year and half that first time around, but it was well worth it, because it was in my first year there that my first conversion occurred –his name was Jay.

***

Jay and I became close friends within a few months of meeting one another. We were inseparable. We went camping, played sports, worked on homework and spent endless hours just talking; you name it, we did it together, including drinking. I had never drunk in high school because drinking was something we were never allowed to do. With an alcoholic dad, it was considered one of the worst things you *could* do. "Do you want to grow up to be like your father?" my mother would yell at us. As if growing up to be like my father was such a bad thing. Drinking was almost as bad as being a "dirty old man" in my house.

And yet, there I was, in college seminary, dressing and acting like a priest during the day and a crazy college student at night. Jay and I would hit the bars with our fake I.D.'s, four or five times a week easy. We also did a lot of touching. Mostly massages and things like that – shoulders, backs, etc. It seemed perfectly normal and appropriate at the time. As the year continued, however, we got closer and closer. Eventually, we would come back from the bars and lay in the same bed together – cuddling and talking about everything, including the Church's teaching on homosexuality and whether or not we wanted to be priests; from time to time we would pray together before we slowly drifted off to sleep.

One night, laying together, fully clothed and cuddling, the direction we were headed became clear. The energy in the room was enormous.

After a few moments, he stopped me and asked, "Are you gay?"

"Are you?"

"I'm not sure, I might be."

After a long pause, I said, "I think I'm gay." And then I started to cry.

After a few silent moments, Jay asked, "Why are you crying?"

"Because I'm not supposed to be gay. It's wrong."

"Who says it's wrong?"

"Everyone – the Church, my parents, everyone."

"No it's not," he said.

"If it's not wrong, then why does everyone say it is?" I asked.

And then Jay said something that forever changed the way I look at myself. He said, "It doesn't matter what everyone else says or thinks. What matters is what *you* say or think...*I don't think it's wrong*."

With those words, my conversion towards self-acceptance began. For the first time, I realized that it really *didn't* matter what anyone else thought, what matters is what I think, and Jay, of course. It was the intimacy we shared that let me see the truth. Had anyone else said that to me, it wouldn't have had the same impact, but because Jay said it, it instantly became true. The single most important voice in my life had validated me as a person – a gay person. He wasn't bothered by it, he wasn't upset, he didn't see anything wrong with it. This cute, eighteen-year-old who I was utterly infatuated with, just said it was okay to be gay, and that's all it took for me to begin to accept myself. I was gay. I knew it now. I also knew that all the stereotypes that I had in my head wouldn't have to apply to me. I could be my own person. I could be the gay person I was meant to be. Acceptance had begun. It would be another couple of years before Jay finally began accepting his own orientation – but eventually he would listen to his own voice and his own truth too.

***

By the end of the first semester my sophomore year, I decided to leave the seminary. I used the words "I want to spread my wings" to tell people why I was leaving, but the truth of the matter was I was deep into drinking and drug use, and seminary nights out just weren't cutting it anymore. I was well on my way to becoming my father, but I didn't know that yet. The two worst things I could be, a gay and a drunk – what would my mother say? Some things can't be avoided, unfortunately, and my years spent drinking are one of them.

After leaving the seminary, I transferred to a state college reputed to be quite the party school. It lived up to its reputation. Though I was meant to be starting my junior year, the transfer left me a semester behind, without a declared major, and with poor enough grades that I needed to make up some of my previous coursework. None of that mattered. Over the next several years, my drinking, drug use and sexual exploration increased at a frantic pace; I just couldn't get enough. I didn't have a problem though, everyone was doing it—right? This was a party school, after all. I didn't realize until years later that everyone was *not* doing it. To me, it seemed like everyone was partying like I was, but that's because I only hung out with the partying type.

By the end of my first semester, I was on academic probation. By the end of my first year, I had a minor criminal record—disturbing the peace, running a disorderly house, that sort of thing. Taking the first offenders program and paying court costs was a quick fix, and the partying continued. My new friends and I partied *all* the time. Pot was almost always available and random hookups were common. While I wasn't out to most of my new friends, I did make a few friends who were gay. These were the people I came out to and these were the ones who showed me the gay scene on campus and in the neighboring cities. I learned a lot from these guys, but I never let my 'mainstream' friends know about this part of my life.

***

After a couple of years, the friends I had began to graduate and move on. The extra semester I got stuck with coming in finally caught up with me. I felt very much alone. It was during this semester that I first began to question the amount of drinking I was doing. In the past, I could always justify my behavior— everyone's doing it! Suddenly, that wasn't the case; there were fewer and fewer people to drink with—might I have a problem?

Somehow, and I really don't know how, I managed to graduate. Degree in hand, I quickly put those sorts of questions behind me, moved back to my home town, got a job and an apartment and found another group of party friends. Over the next six years, this was my life: job found, apartment, job loss, eviction, job found, apartment, job loss, eviction, and on and on, all in combination with anonymous hook ups, pot and booze. Each time the cycle rebooted, it would be harder and harder to find a group of party friends that were my age. I tried dating a few times, but dating for me meant spending the night with the same person more than once. I even tried dating a girl for awhile, don't ask me why, since there wasn't much I wanted from that other than to 'cover' my orientation to my 'mainstream' friends.

Every downward spiral, I would swear off drinking—it took so much energy to recreate myself over and over. In the morning, I'd say never again, never again will I repeat last night; by the next evening, I'd repeat the pattern more profoundly still. Over and over. I tried giving up pot, thinking that would help— it only increased the amount I drank. Finally, after swearing it off one last time – I got drunk again. And then it hit me – the problem wasn't my drinking, per say, the problem was *how much* I drank. I know that sounds utterly ridiculous, but to me it made complete sense. So right then and there, I swore off getting drunk.

A few days later, I was meeting some friends. I was utterly convinced that when the time came, I would leave the bar having only a few. But when the time came, I can remember saying to myself the same thing I had said a thousand times before: "I can quit if I want to, I just don't want to quit right now." And I got completely wasted. The next thing I remember was waking up in my car outside my apartment with the engine still running. I don't even remember how I got there. I crawled into my apartment and passed out.

The next day, in a moment of what I can only call grace, the groundwork for my second conversion was laid. It's hard to explain the feeling of waking up and realizing what had happened the night before, realizing that I had done again what I swore I would never do, realizing that I don't remember how I got home. It's hard to explain the feeling that goes with checking the car to see if maybe there was some damage from an accident that I may have caused and not remembered, of checking the news to see if there were any hit and runs last night reported in the area. Don't get me wrong, I had done all this before, but this time, it bothered me in a way it never had – for some reason, it became imminently clear to me that once I started drinking I couldn't stop. The guilt, shame and remorse were overwhelming. So, I stopped drinking completely – cold turkey, white knuckling as they say.

And white knuckling it was. I was going crazy. Within a few weeks I thought I was headed towards a nervous breakdown. Alcohol withdrawal is nothing to sneeze at. I literally thought I was going to lose my mind. The compulsion to drink and the cravings are overwhelming. And nowhere was safe! Everything was a trigger–going to work, staying at home, watching TV, billboard advertisements, commercials, everything! My whole life had revolved around drinking for so many years that everything I did triggered me to want to drink – it was the closest thing to hell that I have ever experienced.

But even hell loses its power in the face of God's grace—conversion number 2.

A few more weeks of cold turkey later, and I found myself curled up under my desk in my office at home bawling my eyes out. I was speaking to a friend on the phone who knew more about alcoholism than I did. Her advice to me was to go to a meeting with others who shared a desire to stop drinking and who were putting their lives back together – and I did.

I found a fellowship of men and women who had the desire to stop drinking and I attended their meetings. I would come late and leave early – I didn't want anyone to know who I was, the shame of becoming my father was overwhelming—but while I sat in the meetings and listened to people speak, I found a profound sense of serenity. It was the one place I could go in the course of the day that didn't trigger the desire to drink. Alcohol lost its power during those meetings, and I was at peace.

I can remember the first time I said it out loud, the first time they called on me. I introduced myself according to the custom and as I began saying, "…and I'm an alcoholic," I started to sob. It was a release I had not known since that time with Jay so many years before, and it was good. It was as if the weight of the world had been lifted off my shoulders – once again, the truth was setting me free. I was too embarrassed to go back to that meeting for years, but I did find other meetings I would attend on a regular basis. I got with a guy who would mentor me through my early years of sobriety and who helped me discover a life of joy and happiness without drinking. In time, I would also have the privilege of assisting others in their sobriety and recovery.

***

One of the main principles of this fellowship is a relationship with God as you understand him. I would learn that there is no power in the universe strong enough to keep me sober other than God. While lots of people in the fellowship struggle with this concept, it was an easy one for me to grasp. I started going to the local Church and began reconnecting with God. It didn't take long for me to re-establish that relationship – after all, I was once in the seminary. But this time, it was different; I now had a dependency on this relationship. It was personal, and it was survival. I needed God's help. Within a very short time, my relationship with God and my prayer and meditation began bearing fruit.

46

I was taught to ask God to direct my thoughts, to ask for his will to be done in my life – and I did. Almost immediately, thoughts of the priesthood returned. I had tried it before but left to 'spread my wings.' Ten years, two conversions, and a world of experiences later – I would try it again.

***

After a year and a half of recovery, I am out of debt, I have made most of my amends and I have an appointment with the vocation office. I decide I'm going to be brutally honest with them, knowing that there's a good chance they're not going to take me. I am upfront with them about my drinking history, my work history, and my sex history. I lay it all on the line. Once you make it through the interviews with the vocation office, the psychological testing, the medical exams and behavioral examinations, there are more interviews with members of the faculty. In four of the six faculty interviews, they ask about my orientation. Three of these four faculty members ask about my sexual history and I tell them as much as they want to know. All of them ask if I can be celibate, and I reply that I think I can.

The biggest concern they seemed to have was not, surprisingly, regarding my orientation, but rather, my recovery. For some of them, it was too early in my sobriety to be making a big decision; for others, it wasn't clear that I really was done drinking. My acceptance into the seminary was delayed, but after demonstrating continued sobriety, I was allowed to enter the following year.

***

By now, I'm thirty-years-old, and I haven't had a drink in three years. The most important thing for me is my relationship with God and my desire to help others find God more deeply in their lives. In the seminary, I thrive. From time to time, the issue of homosexuality comes up in class, and we're taught the traditional teaching of the Church: 'It's okay to be gay, but not to live in a gay relationship.' While the Church admits that some people are born gay due to no fault of their own, and that there should be no discrimination against them, it nonetheless maintains that living a gay lifestyle is sinful. In other words, having gay sex is a sin.

I found this stance intriguing, so I decided to do my first morality paper on the topic. When I asked the morality professor, a priest, for assistance, he gave me a long list of Catholic theologians who are pushing the envelope regarding the Church's teachings on homosexuality. We have a big, big Church, and there are many ways to interpret its teachings. This professor opened me up to that vastness, he helped me to see that the Church's teaching can be found not only in the hierarchy but also in the voices of those Catholic theologians who struggle to find ways to understand and interpret the truths they have discovered in their own journey with God. It was time well spent, even if the paper wasn't that great.

***

Throughout the seminary formation period, whenever the issue of gay priests was brought up, it was always brought up in the context of celibacy – *can you be celibate?* We talked in class about being celibate, about how to deal with desires and so live celibately. One of the suggestions was to form a support group of priests committed to living their vocation with integrity, to helping one another remain good and holy priests.

A few others and I took this advice to heart; just before we were ordained transitional deacons, we formed such a group. Undoubtedly, this was one of the best decisions

I've ever made. We meet once a month and have been meeting for years. We have never missed a meeting. It is the place I go to be authentic, open, honest, and valued. I don't know how other priests do it without this kind of support. Where do they go when they're struggling? Where do they go when they're frustrated? Who do they tell their secrets to? Perhaps if these sorts of groups were more widely formed, we could have avoided some of the circumstances that led to the 2002 crisis in the first place.

I once heard a piece of advice that I think is worth repeating as often as I can. It is, "We all have a right to privacy, but no one has a right to secrecy." In light of the scandal of 2002, I think this applies more now than ever to the priesthood. We do have a right to privacy, but no priest has a right to secrecy. It's the secrets that get us into trouble. From the hierarchy keeping secrets to the priests keeping secrets – one way or another, it will come back to harm us and harm the Church. Having a place to go that I completely trust and find support in has proven invaluable.

***

My story is like so many others I've heard over the

years: conversion, the discovery of self, the discovery of God, and the growth that comes from building a relationship with each. The truth about myself and God has led me to be who I am today. It is a privileged place, a sacred place. I am a parish priest – perhaps *your* parish priest. I am the priest who ministers to you when your family is breaking apart, the priest who's there for you when your spouse dies, the priest who listens to you when you've lost your job and are struggling. I am the priest who buries your loved ones, who visits you in the hospital or in prison, who helps you get into a treatment program, who helps you try to figure out where God is calling you. I am the priest who brings healing when you've sinned, who lifts you up when you're feeling like a complete failure, who is passionate about preaching the good news, who is willing to listen to your secrets without judgment. I am the priest who helps you accept your orientation, who helps you accept your child's orientation or family member's orientation, who is passionate about helping you get closer to God – the source of all life and love. That's who I am – a priest, your priest, a gay priest.

Chapter Four

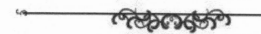

I Am Good at What I Do

I was hesitant to write this chapter at first, but the pervasive story of the troubled gay priest left me with no choice. My intention here is not to brag but to combat the negative stereotypes that abound in today's media. Take, for example, a news story reported by CBS in July, 2010: "Catholic Church Lashes Out at Gay Priest." It quotes a Vatican statement which "lashed out at gay priests who are leading a double life, urging them to come out of the closet and leave the priesthood."[xvi] This statement was issued in response to a published exposé on the double lifestyle of three priests in Rome who were visiting gay bars and spending time with male escorts. Clearly, these men were not living a life of integrity or celibacy. Responding to this CBS report, Bryan Cones, managing editor for *US Catholic* magazine said, "The problem is that only *these* gay priest are the news, not all the other gay priests who labor faithfully, honoring their commitments along with their straight brothers as best they can. We don't hear their stories because they can't tell them for fear of expulsions... I must agree with the Vicar of Rome that it would be helpful if gay priests would come out—so we could thank them for their faithful service, especially as they have been unjustly tarred with "causing" sex abuse.

Unfortunately, our Church leadership at this time is not creating the kind of open and safe space that would allow for such honesty."[xvii] Though there are thousands of us, gay priests who are ministering in the Church and living a life of integrity, honoring our commitments and helping others grow deeper in their faith, our voices have remained hidden. And yet, we *are* here, living, loving, and being who God has called us to be – Catholic priests. I wasn't going to write this; I didn't want to brag. But I can no longer remain silent. I need *you* to hear our stories, the stories of gay priests, good and holy men, ministering in our Church today.

***

I am good at what I do – I know that. But while part of me would love to take all the credit – I can't. The credit belongs to God. The good I do is God working through me, with me and in me. The good I do today is only possible by the grace of God. We (God and I) are good at what we do. And it is that goodness that gives my vocation clarity. There are times when I'm ministering and can see the help I give to someone. It's in those moments that I know I'm doing exactly what God wants me to do. I'm right where God wants me to be. It's no accident that God has called me to the priesthood; it is by God's design, God's plan that I am in this sacred place, this privileged place, this place where I've been blessed to help others grow through their most vulnerable moments, to share their stories with them.

Before I begin telling you a few of these stories, I want you to know that even though many of these people have given me permission to tell their stories, I've changed the details to protect their privacy. I take confidentiality extremely seriously. I would never jeopardize one of the most sacred blessings given to us as priests – a person's trust. People come to us all the time because they trust us. They come to us because they know we won't tell their stories; we won't expose them; we won't call them out. This is indeed a privilege, one that we don't necessarily earn, but it comes with the collar. So please, know that while these stories are true, you will not be able to trace them back to a particular person. Enough said.

Now, for the really tough question, which stories should I tell? I have so many. I thought and prayed for days about which stories to include—stories that deal with homosexuality, other stories of struggle? I don't want to give you the impression that my ministry is all about helping those struggling with gay issues—though I wonder sometimes if it shouldn't be. In fact, I could fill a book telling stories, powerful stories, about how God has used me to help straight couples resolve infidelity, or help straight men addicted to pornography, or help women who've had an abortion, or help teenagers who have gotten pregnant, and on and on. I absolutely love what I do. I love being there in some of the most vulnerable times of a person's life, when they need unconditional love and support to get through a crisis, and I love to give that love with God. The reality is, only a small percentage of my time is spent dealing with those who are struggling with gay issues, but for the purpose of this book, and to give voice to the voiceless, those who are hidden in our Church, I decided to tell you stories related to that struggle.

What follows is representative of the hundreds of stories I could tell, but even these fail to give justice to the breadth of my ministry. As you read, know that every priest I know has similar stories. Mine are not unique— far from it. Multiply what you hear in the next few pages by a hundred and then again by a thousand and you'll begin to get an idea of the amount of good and holiness we priests, gay priests, have fostered in our Church, the amount of God's love we have added to the world.

***

Mark was in middle school at the parish when I first met him. He was part of the group of kids I was hoping would join the youth group after they graduated. His older siblings were already very active in it, having helped shape it into what it was – a safe place for young people to gather and grow deeper in their commitment to God. I would see Mark when I visited his religion class once a week. It was really more of a religion discussion than an actual class, since I'm not much of a teacher in the traditional sense of the word. I prefer to sit and talk with young people about religious issues, letting *them* explore whatever questions they might have. A discussion? I'm all in! Inevitably, things like the Church's teachings on masturbation, birth control, pre-marital sex, divorce and remarriage and, of course, homosexuality came up over the course of a year. It's still stunning to me how exposed our young people are to these topics at an earlier and earlier age. Every one of them had a family member who was remarried outside the Church or was living together with someone outside of marriage or was gay. Their questions were born of their experiences, of their struggles to make sense of what they believed in relation to the Church's teachings.

Needless to say, these religious discussions were difficult at times—particularly when the conversation turned towards issues of homosexuality. I always felt like I had to tiptoe around, being careful with what I said, making sure I didn't say too much or too little. I found that it was easier to give them the Church's teachings along with the teachings of psychologists and other Catholic moral theologians. By doing this, I hoped to give them a more balanced approach to understanding the Church. I always encouraged them to research and pray about these topics on their own as well.

At the end of the day, I would make it clear that any of them could talk with me one-on-one about this issue or any issue which might be on their minds. While I have always said this – it's rare that a young person ever initiate such a conversation immediately. Instead, what I have learned is that they'll wait to initiate that conversation sometime in the future, provided they trust you. And that takes a lot of 'waiting in line.' I spend an

awful lot of time with young people 'waiting in line.'
Let me explain.

***

One day, I was getting ready to go to an amusement
park with a group of teens when the phone rang. My
friend asked me what I was doing and when I told him.
He said, "Haven't you done the amusement park thing
enough? Do you really like the rides that much?"

My response surprised my friend, "No," I said. "I can't
stand the rides, the heat or the crowds. In fact, there is
little I enjoy about it."

"Then why do you go?" asked my friend.

"I go because I get to wait in line. It's while waiting in
line that I get to know the youth and they get to know
me. I get to know what's going on in their lives, what's
important and what they're thinking. Then, someday
down the road, when they really need to talk, they will
know at least one adult who they can trust."

So, a lot of my ministry with youth is 'waiting in line.'
'Waiting in line' at a coffee shop, at a dinner, at a
Church event, you name it. It's just hanging out,

building trust and relationships. It's also a time for them to 'listen to the music' I play.

***

I once heard a talk given by Brian McNaught, in which he wove the phrase, "pay attention to the music you play because people are listening."[xviii] Brian is a motivational speaker who speaks on diversity issues and gives diversity workshops for major corporations. He is a gay man who was fired from his job working for the Catholic Church when he was younger. The "music" he was referring to is not literally music, but the music of our truths, of our way of thinking, of our personalities. Are we inviting and accepting of others or are we cold and harsh to them? Are we welcoming or are we isolating? Will we be frightened by a difference of opinion? It's all music, the music of our lives and our hearts.

As Brian makes a point of saying, people *are* listening to that music. People hear what we play, and they respond accordingly. They know whether or not they can talk to us and even what we might say. If you ask any gay person how and when they decided to come out to someone, they'll tell you that they paid attention to the 'vibe' that person was giving off. Long before someone comes out to another person, they've already heard the music that person plays and received some subtle assurances as to its safety. In a similar way, youth are exceptionally tuned into the music adults' play. They hear it loud and clear. They know if it's safe or not; they know if a particular adult can be trusted. So, waiting in line and playing music is often the best approach to fostering trusting relationships.

***

And this brings me back to Mark. By the time he is old enough to join the youth group, I have been transferred to another parish. I do, however, continue to see him from time to time, usually in the context of his older siblings and family. By the time Mark is a senior in high school, he joins me, his older siblings, and several groups from different parishes on a pilgrimage. It's during this time that Mark and I 'wait in line.' We stay in touch the following year through Facebook, having dinner occasionally. There's a lot of depth to Mark; he's sensitive, creative, and spiritual. One-on-one conversations with him are easy, and there's nothing we don't talk about – well, almost – except the one thing he wants to talk about the most but hasn't gotten up enough courage to do so – I can wait.

When he's a sophomore in college, we go for a long hike. We're walking down a park trail and he's said just about everything except the one thing he wants to say the most. So, I ask him.

"I wonder if it would be helpful for you to just say it. Say what you want to say. Speak it out loud. Name it." There's a long pause. It's coming – I think. But I know better than to push too hard. More pause... And then,

"I'm gay."

After a moment to let it be, to let it sit out in the open, to let it hang in the holiness of the truth those words speak, I say, "Thanks for saying it out loud. You're an amazing person, and I think the world of you. I care about you. Thanks for finally saying it. How are you feeling?"

"Terrified" is his immediate response.

"I'll bet!...I'm here to support you in whatever way I can." What a holy space this is; how privileged I am to be here in this moment.

***

The first time any of us have ever spoken those words out loud have been some of the most difficult yet freeing words of our lives. And, they're only the beginning. Now that Mark knows the truth about himself, he has to figure out what to do with it. Accept it? Reject it? Hide it? Mark begins the journey of acceptance; he begins to experience the freedom of his truth, to be free in ways he's never thought possible, free in ways he could only imagine. Over the next several months (years really), I support Mark in coming out to his family and friends; I help him figure out where God might be calling him. Today, he's one of the more balanced people I know.

***

As true as that is, I am also brutally aware that there are many, many more who don't come out to the clergy because of the hierarchy's anti-gay campaign. I call it a campaign because, since the scandal of 2002, the hierarchy has deliberately and systematically attacked the homosexual community. We have, as a Church, driven away thousands of our members, gay and straight alike. Even gay-friendly Catholic communities struggle to keep gay members. I am doing what I can in my small part of the world, but every day it's getting more and more difficult to be Catholic and gay. There just doesn't seem to be a place in the pews for us anymore. Can anyone be blamed for asking, should I find a new place?

And yet I stay, encouraged by the stories of those who refuse to leave for love of the Church, a love that I share. A few years back, I remember hearing one such story during a talk by Gregory Maguire, the author of "Wicked". His words have helped me through. Gregory, for those who do not know, is a gay man, legally married, with several adopted children. He is also Catholic. He was raised Catholic and has many, many fond memories of his faith. He tells the story that, when he and his husband were deciding to adopt, the only requirement he had was that they raise their kids Catholic. And so they raise their children Catholic today.

By and large, Gregory has found acceptance from the Catholic community where he and his family worship. In his talk, however, he addressed the ongoing struggle he and so many others like him continue to have with the hierarchy, focusing on one of the recent statements about the 'violence' gay couples cause to the children they adopt. His outrage was visceral. How dare they try to push him out! He was raised Catholic and loves the Catholic Church. And so, he had this to say: "I have been inspired by Rosa Parks who one day decided to not give up her seat on the bus. Inspired by this courage, I will not give up my place in the pew."[xix]

I hold firmly to those words, especially during times when I feel frustrated, burned by the hierarchy. *I will not give up my place in the pew.* Don't we all have a place in the pew? Isn't that part of the gospel message we profess? Black or white, gay or straight, divorced or married, legal or undocumented immigrant, all of us, every one of us, has a place in the pew. It saddens me to watch so many of our Catholic brothers and sisters leave the Church because they no longer feel like that place exists. I completely understand—sometimes I wonder if I have a place—and yet, I know with an unbreakable certainty, that right now God has called me to his priesthood, has called me to hold that place in the pew with everything I've got. For as long as I have a place, others will have a place. The Marks of our Church will have a place. All of God's children will have a place in the pew.

***

I'd like to take a moment to introduce you now to Barb. I was assigned to a typical, upper-middle income parish when I got a call from the public high school principal asking if I would come up to the school and help minster to the students. It had just been discovered that one of the students had committed suicide, sending shockwaves through the campus. The principal had made the library available to any students who wanted to talk, write, cry or to just be. I arrived at the library to find several dozen kids hanging out—some upset, some angry, some with questions, others crying. It's a great idea to give high school students a place to go when tragedy hits their community. In the hours I spent there, I only saw a handful of my own parishioners. Most of the kids were of other faith traditions, including the youth who committed suicide – or so I thought.

***

Several weeks later, one of my parishioners brought a friend by my office for a talk. Her friend was Barb, the twin sister of the boy who had committed suicide; she wasn't at the school the day the others found out about her brother's suicide, and she had a lot to process. Barb and I were alone for a long time – lots of tears, lots of hurt, and lots of anger were expressed. Over the course of the conversation, it came out that she and her family *were* once practicing Catholics, though they had fallen away from the Church sometime after her first communion. It wasn't an abrupt change but a gradual drifting away—Church didn't seem important anymore. Their family just didn't need God in their lives – until now. In that moment, at that time in her life, Barb needed God more than anyone I knew.

I started meeting with her on a regular basis, and for the longest time there were mostly tears. Over the next several months, however, we began to talk. First, about her brother and how much she missed him, and then about her and how she was getting by. The conversion which began in her many months before was beginning to bear fruit. She started coming back to Church, receiving again the sacraments of reconciliation and the Eucharist for the first time in years. It was an amazing experience to watch her grow into her dependency on God. Though her grief was profound, she was moving towards acceptance.

On the anniversary of her brother's death, she came to

visit with some pictures. As we were looking at them, she told me more about him. I can't remember what exactly she said, but it was how she said it that made me wonder if her brother hadn't been gay. Up until now, why he committed suicide was a mystery to all of us. There was no note, no signs of depression, no indication that he was having a difficult time in school or with his friends; there was nothing. His suicide had shocked everyone, including his sister. Very gently, I asked her if she had ever thought about whether or not her brother might have been gay. Her tears gave me the answer. More healing, more forgiveness, more support and more love. We would, in the months ahead, talk about her brother's orientation and affirm her willingness to love him for who he was.

***

The Suicide Prevention Resource Center estimates that over thirty percent of all LGBT teenagers have attempted suicide by the time they turn 21.[xx] Over thirty percent – that's staggering to me. If ever there were a time the Church should be welcoming towards gay people, it is now. Think about how many lives could be saved if the Church would have a loving, caring, welcoming attitude towards homosexuals. The issue of homosexuality is not just an issue for theological debate; it's a matter of life and death. For better or for worse, what the hierarchy says matters, it impacts the world in both positive and negative ways, as the stories above bare witness.

***

I recently watched a compelling documentary called "For the Bible Tells Me So," which investigates just how harmful a fundamentalist approach can be to gay children. This sort of approach takes a select few Bible verses literally, citing them as "proof" that homosexuality is an abomination. In the film, we hear the stories of parents who have lost their children to suicide, children who were unable to find the acceptance that they needed to survive. These parents now work for organizations that support love and tolerance among all of God's people.

Love and tolerance – shouldn't we all be working towards that? When the hierarchy speaks as it does against the civil rights of gay people, it too contributes to the bigotry and oppression against us. Our hierarchy, as it presently stands, is on the wrong side of this movement – it's that simple. As a matter of justice, discrimination needs to be condemned.

Towards the end of the documentary, Bishop Desmond Tutu is quoted as saying, "I can't for the life of me imagine that God would say...'I punish you because you are homosexual, you ought to have been heterosexual.' I can't, I can't for the life of me believe that that is how God sees things." [xxi] At the end, God won't ask, "What is your orientation?" He'll ask, "What have you done for the least of my brothers and sisters?"" For the marginalized? For the oppressed? For those yearning for a love as yet un-given? That is what God will be asking us at the end of our lives, that is what Jesus communicates to us in the scripture passage that separates the sheep from the goats.

And that is where I struggle the most. Am I doing enough to end injustice and bigotry against gay people? I'll hear about a young man who was beaten to death by a group of boys because he was gay, or a group of gays who were beaten after leaving a bar. I'll hear about a foreign country who wants to condemn a person to death because he or she is gay. I'll hear about a teenager who, for no apparent reason, commits suicide, and I'll wonder

71

if that's why he did it, because he could not find a place that would accept him, a place that would love him for who he is – a place in the pew, in anyone's pew. These, the voices of those who suffer, those who have been oppressed, they haunt me from time to time. Am I really doing enough?

By hiding my voice I know that, at least in some small way, I am contributing to the oppression and bigotry which exists in our society and our Church. At the same time, however, my vocation to the priesthood has never been clearer. I am good at what I do. I know that God has called me to the priesthood, that he wants me to be here now, to support the Marks and the Barbs of this world. I take some satisfaction in knowing that as a priest in active ministry I have the access I need to help those who are struggling with this and other issues. If I were to leave or be asked to leave, that would change dramatically. Other doors would certainly open, but the access I currently have to the Marks and Barbs of this world would be gone. So I stay, with the thousands of other gay priests who love our Church and have dedicated ourselves to it. I stay, hoping that my presence will do more good than my silence will do harm. I stay, trying to give a voice to the truth I've discovered. For now – I stay.

Chapter Five

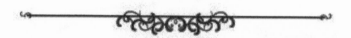

Bash

'Bash' is defined by Merriam-Webster dictionary as "to attack physically or verbally."[xxii] Today, hierarchy-supported attacks on those perceived to be gay, or 'gay bashing,' is on the rise. This causes immeasurable harm to the laity and the priesthood alike, from our youth struggling to find a place in the pews to the seminarian struggling with his sexuality. One of my main concerns is with regard to the process of seminary formation today, the wellbeing of our future priests. A growing hostility has furthered the scapegoating of gay priests begun by the hierarchy in its 2005 statement denying gay men ordination to the priesthood; it has turned many seminaries into un-safe places where open and regular gay bashing occurs. This atmosphere of hostility is leading many seminarians to repress rather than discover their sexual identities, a reality that is particularly damaging given the young and impressionable age of most seminarians. I have already begun to see the negative effects this has had on several well-intended, good men as they try to figure out God's calling in their lives. It saddens me deeply that the attitude towards gays in the seminary has changed so dramatically in the last six years. I'm sickened by it. While I have been able to help a few of these seminarians, it is my prayer that the others find the support they need to accept and discover the truth about themselves.

***

I remember when the Vatican's statement refusing to ordain gay men to the priesthood first came out in 2005. There was a lot of emotion surrounding the document in the months leading up to its release. It was in these months that many of my priest brothers and I gathered to talk about our frustrations and concerns, struggling to form an appropriate response. After much discussion and thought, I decided I needed to come out publicly. For weeks I drafted a letter to parishioners. The exercise of writing that letter gave me the opportunity to give voice to my feelings about the Church and its statement, and it ultimately led to this book. That letter, however, still sits on the bookshelf in my office, waiting for the postman. Perhaps someday.

***

Since 2005, I've read and re-read that Vatican document many times. Needless to say, I am still not a fan. This document and the hierarchy's efforts to scapegoat gay priests for the 2002 scandal are among the main reasons seminaries have become such hostile places today. The way in which seminarians and faculty openly 'bash' the gay culture is driving those students who are gay further into the closet. I am told by gay and straight seminarians I know that it is not uncommon to overhear students ridiculing the gays as they protest a particular civil rights issue. Such bashing is public, encouraged through the silence, if not outright support, of the administration. This was not the attitude present when I was in the seminary. Don't get me wrong, I did witness my fair share of bashing, but it never went unchallenged. Someone would have spoken up and said, "Hey, have a little compassion" or something. But not today – the culture of hostility has come with a culture of fear. Students are afraid to challenge gay bashing; they're afraid to say anything for fear of being labeled gay themselves. When I asked a straight seminarian why he didn't speak out, he said, "I was too afraid." It takes a lot of courage to stand up for what is just in the face of fear, to speak out against injustice—shouldn't we be teaching that to our seminarians rather than its opposite?

***

While I have referenced the effects of this 2005 Vatican

document throughout my book, I think it's important, at this point, to examine it more closely in order to have a context from which to speak about the current Church attitude towards homosexuality going forward. Entitled "Instruction Concerning the Criteria for the Discernment of Vocations with regard to Persons with Homosexual Tendencies in view of their Admission to the Seminary and to Holy Orders," this document basically affirms that, "it contains norms concerning a specific question, made more urgent by the current situation, and that is: whether to admit to the seminary and to holy orders candidates who have deep-seated homosexual tendencies."[xxiii] It goes on to explain that the Church "cannot admit to the seminary or to holy orders those who practice homosexuality, present deep-seated homosexual tendencies or support the so-called 'gay culture'."[xxiv] And, "One must in no way overlook the negative consequences that can derive from the ordination of persons with deep-seated homosexual tendencies."[xxv] "Different, however," the Congregation says, "would be the case in which one were dealing with homosexual tendencies that were only the expression of a transitory - for example, that of an adolescence not yet superseded. Nevertheless, such tendencies must be clearly overcome at least three years before ordination to the diaconate."[xxvi] Finally, the document notes, citing the catechism, that "although the particular inclination of the homosexual person is not a sin, it is a more or less strong tendency ordered toward an intrinsic moral evil; and thus the inclination itself must be seen as an objective disorder," enough to disqualify a candidate for the priesthood.[xxvii]

So, there it is in a nut shell. Basically and in laymen's terms, the Church is telling us two main things. First, that it cannot ordain gay men to the priesthood but can allow those who are 'transitory gay' to enter the priesthood provided they have overcome their tendencies and been chaste for three years. The document's allowances make an interesting distinction between gay and transitory gay here. Someone who is 'curious' or 'bi', who may have experimented in adolescence but is not 'really' gay can be ordained after just three years, but a gay person with deep-seated homosexual tendencies or one who has the inclination towards homosexuality (which is not a sin in and of itself, according to this very document) remains forever unfit for ministry, end of story. It's a ridiculous claim, I know, but there it is.

Perhaps even more disturbing and insulting than that claim, however, is the Church's second one. Here, in written word, we find the Church attempting to scapegoat gay men for the problems the hierarchy created in the massive cover up of pedophilia which took place for decades. The lines, "made more urgent by the current situation" and "one must in no way overlook the negative consequences that can derive from the ordination of persons with deep-seated homosexual tendencies, are clearly alluding to the pedophilia crisis, subtly blaming gay priest for those problems. Does the hierarchy really believe the people of God will buy this? Do they really believe that the people are that naïve? Do they really believe that the scandal was caused by the ordination of gay men to the priesthood? I don't think so. The truth of the matter is, the hierarchy needed to shift the blame, and gay priests fit the bill.

***

Fortunately, more and more of us are waking up to this reality. Every intelligent person I have spoken to about this issue understands and is offended by the hierarchy's deliberate attempt to scapegoat gay priests. And so am I. This is not the way to rebuild our reputation and regain the trust of the people. In fact, it's just the opposite. We look even more ridiculous than before. We have lost our credibility. When we put out statements like this, we give further evidence to the people of God that we don't know what they're talking about. We cause more harm than good.

Responding to the 2005 document, Archbishop Bruce J. Simpson, O.S.J.B., wrote, "The continuing misunderstanding of sexuality whereby a gay male is seen as a pedophile will continue to cause great harm to the Roman Catholic Church."[xxviii] Great harm indeed.

While most of us have not bought into the scapegoating, too many in the seminary have. I got a text one day from a gay seminarian after one of his classes. The text outlined the above teachings and the priest added at the end of his class this question: "Could the pedophilia cases have been prevented if this document were in effect years ago? You be the judge." And class was dismissed. You be the judge. At least he got that right. I texted back, "Well, sounds like *you* get to be the judge." In later conversations, we spoke about the anger and hurt caused by these kinds of statements. They're unjust and immoral, and they are damaging our

82

seminarians.

***

A few years ago, I met a seminarian who was bright, talented, caring and, you guessed it, gay. He had discovered this while at seminary and come to accept it, in a sense. His acceptance was not as a gift from God, however, but as an objective disorder, a cross to bear, a burden given by God for him to carry through life. In his mind, if the inclination he has to love a person of the same sex ever materialized, it would be a sin of the gravest sort.

It'd been years since I'd met a person so ashamed of their orientation. When I asked him what the worst possible thing he could imagine was, he said it was that someone would think he's gay. Because of this, he had only ever come out to two people. In our meeting, I could tell he wanted so desperately to believe, like so many of us believe, but he just couldn't seem to get there – he was intrinsically disordered. The hierarchal voices in his head came to him at an impressionable and vulnerable time in his life, dominating his thoughts, overpowering that much quieter voice, a voice deep down, the voice of truth which so desperately wanted him to accept and believe that there was nothing wrong with him, that he was already loved. The Church believes being gay is wrong, that it is against nature and natural law; as long as you believe that too, you can never fully embrace and love who you are. It saddens me to report, that though this young man has had a few tiny breakthroughs, the hierarchal voice and authentic voice within remain unresolved; self-acceptance continues to elude him. I pray that the truth will one day set him free. Our Church teaching, complicated by the scapegoating of gay priests, has made it all too easy for seminarians to repress their sexuality and suffer the consequences.

***

I got a call one day from a person I'd never met who lived across the country. She represented an organization that sponsored a workshop I once attended on the promotion of positive Church teachings regarding homosexuality. At the time, this organization also received, with some regularity, calls and emails from priests and laypeople struggling to accept themselves as gay and Catholic. One of the calls they had received came from a gay priest who was passing through my area and needed to talk. I immediately agreed.

It was an awesome meeting. I was the first person this priest had the courage to come out to face-to-face. Prior to this, he had only come out via email and phone. He was in his fifties and had finally accepted his orientation. As we got to talking, he began to recall how, when he was in seminary, they were taught, gay and straight alike, to 'repress' any sexual urges that they may have had. He had been taught not to engage any fantasy or any sexual urge whatsoever. That had, he reflected, led him to a life of repression and denial. His attractions were so repressed, in fact, that when he finally shared them with me, it scared him so much that he cried. I can remember feeling so incredibly sorry for him. He felt cheated and used by the Church. Cheated, because now that he was in his fifties, he was just beginning to understand who he was. Used, because now that he knew himself to be gay and was considering taking some time off to explore what that meant to him, he had no real options. After more than twenty-five years of service to the Church, walking away now meant walking away with nothing – no retirement, no savings, nothing at all. Having given himself to the Church for so long, he was left feeling scared, alone, sad, and angry; he was a lost man trying to figure out what to do with the rest of his life.

***

After all that I have said, you may have wondered why more gay priests just don't leave the Church. Can you imagine the courage it would take at the age of fifty-five to walk away from what you've known your entire adult life? There are no unemployment benefits (as a non-profit the Church doesn't have to pay into unemployment). There are no retirement benefits, no 401k's, nothing at all waiting for you. While some priest have begun creating their own retirement accounts, most of the priests I know have nothing personally set aside, and to be honest, we don't get paid enough to make any real contribution towards such a plan anyway. A priest's retirement generally consists of living in a parish as a 'senior associate' and collecting social security. Given the way social security works, however – the lower your income, the lower your benefit –the average priest can only count on between $600 and $800 in benefits each month. That's awful. And, there is no health insurance if you leave. None. At the age of 55, you can imagine how frightening that might be. In short, a priest who leaves has no place to live, no retirement, no health insurance, and best of all, they can't be employed by the Church. The jobs that they would be most qualified to have they're not eligible for because they are no longer priests in active ministry. As you can tell, leaving the priesthood is a frightening prospect, to say the least.

I have thought about this and believe if the Church was actually serious about wanting gay priests to leave, they would need to create a severance package to give us a chance to get on our feet, to make it on our own. But that just may be the point. The hierarchy might not *want* us to leave. To use us as a scapegoat is one thing, but to have us leave active ministry, why, that would send shockwaves through the entire system. There are simply too many of us in active ministry today. When the 2005 document came out, I can remember seeing a cartoon in the paper which had in the first frame, a picture of the Pope promulgating to a group of priests: "The Church will no longer ordain gay men to the priesthood." And in this frame, the priests are all leaving the room. In the next frame, you can see the Pope saying, "No, not you guys, I mean any *new* priests." And the priests are all coming back into the room. If any significant population of gay priests ever left the Church at one time, it would change the face of the Church forever – which is why I believe the Church doesn't make it easier for priests to leave and recreate their lives outside of ministry. You have to remember that the gay priests I'm speaking about haven't done anything wrong, they're simply trying to figure out if they have a place in the pew. I've often thought about creating a safe house or a non-profit organization to assist ex-priests in getting on their feet. Until someone does, however, the fear of leaving active ministry is quite real.

All of that said, I am proud to report that the traveling priest I spoke with finally did find the courage to leave active ministry for a while. Though we haven't been in touch for some time now, I've learned that after several years away from active ministry, he has returned and, at least for now, has found a place in the pew. He has come to accept the truth about himself, a truth which for too many remains repressed and deep within, but one that, once surfaced, can lead to a life of great freedom and authenticity.

***

The hierarchy's efforts to scapegoat gay priests has led

to a hostile environment towards homosexuality in our Church. Whether we are talking about the ordination of gay men to the priesthood or gay marriage or any number of other issues, the hierarchy continuously lashes out against the gay community. This hostility has created an atmosphere of gay bashing in seminaries, forcing more and more gay seminarians into the closet, further away from accepting their truth. The consequences of repression will be devastating to those individuals and to our Church in the years to come. I pray every day for those struggling, both in and out of our seminaries, to accept their homosexuality – please join me in my prayer.

Chapter Six

What I want to Say

Believe it or not, it's not easy to stay hidden. It's not easy to stay hidden at a time in our country's history when civil rights for gays is finally gaining momentum. It's not easy to stay hidden when there's so much good I could be doing to promote acceptance in our country. It's not easy to stay hidden, closeted and quiet when there's a message that needs to be heard. I suppose, in some way, that's what this book is really about – it's my attempt to share that message, to give gay priests a voice by sharing what they and many straight priests believe regarding homosexuality.

Even as I share this truth here, however, I stay in some ways hidden, and the struggle continues, deep and intense inside me. Should I come out publicly and possibly lose my place in active ministry? I've been dealing with this struggle for years now – and there's no end in sight. My greatest fear is that when my time comes and I stand before God, God will ask, "Why didn't you speak the truth that I gave you to speak?" And whatever answer I give, it won't be adequate.

And that's really it. I've been given a truth to speak, but I cannot speak it. It's a struggle for me and for every gay priest that I know. It's a struggle we each have to try and make peace with in our own way. And it's a struggle between goods – do we stay hidden and do the good work that so many of us are doing as ministers of the Church, or do we come out and do the good work of speaking the truth about homosexuality? There really is no clear answer. On the one hand, the good we do in our parishes is enormous. In the short time I've been a priest, I've seen firsthand all the good that can be done by men of integrity as we live out our vocations. That's a lot of good to turn away from. On the other hand, so much good could be done by coming out, by helping reshape people's minds and attitudes towards gays, especially in the Church. It's a struggle between goods, with all of us stuck trying to figure out which good God wants us to do. How can our response be adequate?

I recently told some friends of mine, "I'm tired of struggling. I just want to be at peace. I haven't been at peace for a very long time – and I want to be at peace." While I know my efforts to write this book aren't going to be the complete answer, they are, at least for now, allowing me an opportunity to give voice to the truth. There is much I want to say about the truth I have discovered. While these words are my words, I know that they echo the attitudes and beliefs of many loving priests, both gay and straight. I am but one voice representing thousands who share these beliefs.

***

So, what *do* I want to say?

I want to say that homosexuality is a gift from God that can lead to life-giving, committed relationships of love. Often, these unions lead to parenting and the raising of children in a loving, nurturing, and caring environment. The truth is, there is nothing intrinsically disordered or wrong about homosexuality – it is different than heterosexuality, but it is not deficient. This is what I want to say.

And I've said it to lots of people, lots of times. I've said it in countless counseling sessions with individuals and in small Church communities. I've said it to young gay adolescents who are struggling with their orientation. But when it comes to publicly speaking this truth from the pulpit, I have not said it. I have implied it, when I preach love, tolerance and acceptance of all people, when I preach against bullying, discrimination or hatred of any kind, but I have not said it directly. I have remained hidden.

Martin Luther King Jr. once said, "We will have to repent in this generation, not merely for the hateful words and actions of the bad people, but for the appalling silence of the good people."[xxix] There are times when my silence appalls me.

***

I believe that as equal rights for gay people continue to make the headlines across our country, there will be a growth in the anti-gay movement as well. We have already seen this play out in the media. We see gay people struggling for equality at work and at home, with anti-gay movements escalating in parallel. It reminds me of the civil rights movement of the 1960's, only this time, the Church is defending the wrong side. I once heard Sister Helen Prejean, author of "Dead Man Walking", say, "The next civil rights movement we face in this country will be among the gay community."[xxx] And she's right, of course. It's happening right now.

Every day in the news, we hear more and more about the anti-gay movement in schools, where gay bullying is rampant. From school administrations, to school boards, to teachers in the classrooms, gay bullying has been tolerated, resulting in the deaths of many students like

Barb's brother. An increase in teenage suicide has been linked to gay bullying, and the gay community has responded.

One of my favorite responses to this has been the "It Gets Better" campaign. This campaign, featured on YouTube and Facebook, has famous and influential people speaking directly to at-risk teenagers saying quite simply, "It gets better."[xxxi] I love this because it reaches out directly to teenagers who are struggling with their orientation and acceptance, assuring them that it does, in fact, get better. And it does. It may not seem that way, especially to a teenager or adolescent who faces bullying and bigotry every day, but it's true – it gets better. It gets better through acceptance. It gets better the moment we begin accepting the truth, the moment we accept ourselves and others – it gets better. This is what I want to say. Acceptance is the key to happiness and freedom.

***

There was a time in my life, at the beginning of my second conversion, when I'd forgotten how to pray. At that time, I was working at an office approximately forty minutes away from where I lived. That gave me at least an hour and a half alone in the car each day. Unsure of what else to do with that time, I began using it to pray as best I could. When I told one of my friends about this undertaking, she suggested that I pray the Serenity Prayer: "God, grant me the serenity to accept the things I cannot change. Courage to change the things I can, and the wisdom to know the difference."[xxxii] She thought I should pray it over and over again, as a mantra, a meditation, applying it to different situations in my life. I did, and the results were awesome.

Though I had prayed this prayer since my childhood, I had never prayed it like that. An hour and half every day, I said the prayer, over and over, meditating on it, thinking about particular situations in my life, discerning what the prayer meant and how it applied to those areas. The first thing I noticed was just how much more peaceful my rush hour experience became. The other drivers kept doing the crazy things they had always been doing, but they stopped bothering me as I began to accept them. The very fact that I was in rush hour traffic in the first place stopped bothering me as I began to accept it. Soon enough, I accepted the fact that in order to get to work on time and with less stress, I would have to leave ten minutes earlier. I was used to waiting to the last possible moment to leave and then spending the next forty minutes under pressure trying to get to work. As I continued meditating on and applying the Serenity Prayer to other areas of my life, life got better – because my acceptance of life got better. In the end, I began to realize that there is so very little in this world that I can change – I'm just not that powerful, and that's okay.

Eventually, I prayed this prayer and applied it to my orientation, discovering a much deeper, more profound level of acceptance and peace. I had known I was gay for many years, and had accepted my orientation for the most part, but there was still some part of me that wanted to change it. I wanted to be like everyone else. Through this prayer, God gave me the wisdom I had been seeking – God gave me the truth. There was nothing I could do to change who I was. I was who I was. I was the person God created me to be. I could not change it. My orientation was not a choice – it was a gift. A gift I had discovered through acceptance.

***

I want to say that homosexuality is not a choice. I think much of our society is coming around to accepting this, but we've still got a long way to go. It used to be that we would speak about homosexuality as a preference –

as if someone prefers same-sex over opposite-sex relationships. It just isn't that way. You don't simply develop a taste for same-sex one day like you would a vanilla latte or a peach pie. Homosexuality is not a choice.

If it were, who would choose it? Who would choose a life of discrimination, bigotry, harassment, bashing and bullying? No, homosexuality is not a choice. Even the Church has accepted this – "Some persons find themselves through no fault of their own to have a homosexual orientation." [xxxiii]

There *is* a choice to be made, however. It's not choosing whether or not to be gay, it's choosing whether or not to accept that you *are* gay. Gay people have to choose to accept their orientation. Heterosexual people have to choose to accept homosexuals. Choosing your orientation is not a choice, but choosing to accept it is. Homosexuality is a gift that we can and should accept and embrace. This is what I want to say.

***

Unfortunately, there are those who would strongly disagree with what I just said, those who believe against all evidence to the contrary that homosexuality *is* a choice. They believe that through treatment and prayer, someone can change their orientation enough to live what they perceive to be a healthy, normal and "straight" life. Those who believe this have spent millions of dollars creating re-orientation camps and retreat centers around the country to take on willing (and sometimes unwilling) participants in an effort to change them. These groups claim they have had much success in helping people become straight through conversion therapy. As you might imagine, I don't support these efforts.

While I've not met many people who have gone through these sorts of programs, I want to share the story of one, a man I met shortly after his "treatment." At the time, he was dating a girl in my parish. On the surface, the treatment looked like it had worked. However, there was another side to him – a secret life of cruising parks, bathhouses and clubs, a secret life of anonymous and high-risk sexual behaviors that was compulsive and out of control. We began meeting on a regular basis, uncovering the different layers of repression and working towards acceptance. We made some progress, but he eventually stopped coming to see me. I'm not sure how he is today, though I think about and pray for him often.

My prayer, for him and others like him, is the Serenity Prayer. I pray that someday, they will find the peace and serenity that comes from acceptance. The thing I remember most clearly about this young man is that he wanted so desperately to be like everyone else, but no matter how hard he tried, he just wasn't. Repressing his homosexuality only led him to a life of risk that he never thought he would be living. We've all seen this type of repression played out in the lives of famous people like politicians, evangelists and clergy, those who get caught trying to have sex in public bathrooms, or with male prostitutes, or in any number of other risky situations. On the surface, repressed persons can seem like model citizens, living respectable lives, but in secret, they are having sex in some of the least respectable places. They are willing to risk everything they built themselves up to be because they can no longer stand to repress their orientations – the truth inevitably comes out one way or another, be it in healthy or unhealthy ways.

While I know the person I just told you about does not represent everyone who has gone through one of these programs, I can tell you that from what I've read and from my own experience, long-lasting serenity and peace does not come from repression or reorientation but acceptance. Homosexuality is not a choice. This is what I want to say.

***

I also want to say that homosexuality is not an objective disorder. It is not a cross to bear. It is not deficient in any way. Homosexuality is a gift. Far too often, I'll hear well-intended but naïve people compare homosexuality to diabetes or alcoholism—"It's not their fault they're gay, just like it's not someone's fault that they have diabetes or alcoholism, it's genetic." This argument drives me crazy. Untreated diabetes and alcoholism are a death sentence. Untreated homosexuality is not. It needs no treatment. There is no deficiency. Unlike alcoholism and diabetes, homosexuality is not deficient in any way. A gay person doesn't require medicine or treatment—they require acceptance. In fact, the only negative consequences of homosexuality are born not from within the person but from those around him or her. It's what others do and say that causes harm, not the person herself or himself.

A gay person is able to love, live and grow in every way a straight person is able to love, live and grow. We are only free, truly free, when we choose to live as God intended us to live. Homosexuality is not deficient.

***

Contrary to this belief is the hierarchy's supposition that though gays and lesbians do not "choose" to experience same-sex attractions, due to the nature of their orientation, they are, in fact, "sexually disordered." As such, they are called to lead chaste lives. Put otherwise, because homosexual acts are immoral, gay people should be chaste. I disagree. To say all homosexual acts are immoral is to deny the countless experiences of homosexual persons living in life-giving relationships of love with one another. This is what I want to say.

Over the past several years, I have seen many Catholic dioceses create support groups for gay persons and their families. While some of these groups encourage openness and acceptance, many of them lead with Church teachings that try to foster lifelong chastity among gay persons. I have encountered many people who have been part of these sorts of groups at some point in their lives, people who have really tried to live according to those teachings. I have never, however, met anyone who has stayed with them for an extended period of time. Eventually and inevitably, the struggle between what they know to be true and what the Church says is true is too difficult, and they leave, disappointed, frustrated, feeling let down. Many stay conflicted for years to come, while others accept the voice of truth within and live in accordance to how God created them.

***

Last year, I spoke to a gay couple who had been trying to live the Church's teaching by being celibate in their relationship. The conflict and unrest it created in their lives nearly drove them apart. At the time, they had been together for ten years, most of it happy and fulfilled. However, in recent years, when they had been trying to practice chastity – and I say trying – things had collapsed. They would have several successful months together, but then the desire to be physically intimate would take over and they would fail in their commitment to chastity.

After listening to their struggle, I finally asked them; "Do you feel called to chastity?" No one had ever asked them that question before. "The Church says 'because you are gay you are called to chastity,' but do you feel called, do you believe you are called to chastity?"

Eventually, the truth came out – "No," they said, "we don't."

"Then why are you being chaste?" I asked. "The conflict you're experiencing comes from not being authentic to who you are. You are trying to live in a way that is contrary to and does not support who you are. When any of us live that way, we are disintegrated. Integrity is living authentically who we are and who we are called to be. If you are not called to chastity, don't be chaste."

Since then, I have run into them a couple of times, and they are doing much better living the life and love that God has called them to. The peace and freedom they found through acceptance is truly amazing.

***

This is what I want to say. We are only free, truly free, when we choose to live as God intended us to live. Homosexual persons *can* live in life-giving relationships of love with one another. I recently came across an article posted on the New Ways Ministry website.[xxxiv]

New Ways Ministry is dedicated to a gay-positive ministry of advocacy and justice for the LBGT community. The article quotes Austrian Cardinal Christopher Schonborn in May of 2010 as saying: "We should give more consideration to the quality of homosexual relationships. A stable relationship is certainly better than if someone chooses to be promiscuous."[xxxv] He went on to say that the Church ought to respect long-term, committed relationships between people of the same gender. Well said. And at the same time, it saddens me to think that in a Church with hundreds of well-educated and well-intended Cardinals and members of the hierarchy, only one has publically spoken this truth.

It *is* possible to have and live in a life-giving relationship of love, physically, emotionally and spiritually as a gay person. God's love is infinitely capable of growing and fostering a loving relationship between persons of the same sex. One of my favorite definitions for love comes from Pope John Paul II's theology of the body, which says Love is a mutual gift between persons. "The communion of persons means existing in a mutual 'for,' in a relationship of mutual gift."[xxxvi] As a mutual gift, each person has to be free to give of themselves to the other, and each person has to be free to receive what the other person gives. This is what creates unity. If I'm not willing to give of myself or receive what another person is giving, then there can be no unity. It is what St. Paul tries so hard to convey in his writings about becoming the one body of Christ. There can be no unity if I won't receive the gift of another. If I place conditions on which persons I receive in love, then I foster disunity and division rather than oneness. In committed relationships of love, two persons, regardless of orientation, freely and mutually give themselves to each other and receive in turn what the other person gives. This is what God intended, a mutual relationship of love, a gift of self freely given, relationship. Homosexuality is not a curse and it is not a cross – it is as God meant it to be, a gift, an opportunity to love and to share one's life in love with God.

Having said all of that, it will come as no surprise that gay persons, like straight persons, living in committed relationships of love want to extend that love, to share it by having and raising children. Because love is an expression of God, it is generative, it is life-giving, leading many gay couples to seek out ways to have and raise children of their own. As you may have guessed, the hierarchy is opposed to this, saying that gay parents raising children will cause violence and irreversible harm. Appalling! There is plenty of research available that has concluded there is no harm done to children who are raised by gay parents in loving and nurturing environments. Gay couples have been raising children for years. The criteria for causing harm to children is not one's orientation but how one treats them. Raising children in a loving home is the key to raising balanced and emotionally-developed adults. If you disagree, simply meet a gay couple raising children and discover for yourself the incredible gift of God's love being shared between them as well as the struggles all parents face when raising children.

***

There is a song I often listen to which has inspired me to speak the truth more boldly and courageously. The song is "Did Galileo Pray?" by Ellis Paul. I came across the song while researching for a homily that dealt with courage and truth. The song speaks about the experiences of Galileo Galilei, the scientist who courageously spoke the truth he was given to speak, even at penalty of death before the Inquisition; even when a "lie was demanded," Galileo spoke "a truth that every flower which follows the sun, has known all along, what God had done, as they whisper the truth in the seasons that give way."[xxxvii]

There are a few lines of that song that haunt and inspire me even today. "The truth will march in Birmingham and will block the tanks in Tiananmen" is one of them.[xxxviii] Some of the most courageous moments in history have been when individuals commit themselves to speaking the truth through their actions, when individuals join together to stand up for what they believe, to stand up for what is right, to stand up for justice as we are called to today.

There's another line that says, "Neither the Church nor the Pope can deny the Milky Way."[xxxix] This line gives me hope. Hope that someday, the Church hierarchy will stop denying the truth about homosexuality, that someday the Church will look back on its teaching about homosexuality much in the same way as it now looks back on its teaching about geocentrism. I have to have hope, hope that the truth will prevail, hope that the truth will come out, hope that the truth will one day set us free.

***

What I want to say. That's where I began this chapter, giving voice to the truth God has given me to speak. In concluding, I want to say, especially to those who are struggling with accepting their orientation, that you are a beautiful child of God, created in the image and likeness of God, and that there is nothing wrong with you. You are beautiful and holy just the way you are, and if anyone tells you differently, don't listen. *You are beautiful and holy just the way you are.* And no one, not the Catholic Church, not the synagogues or mosques, not the evangelicals, not the kids in school or their parents, not your family or friends can convince you otherwise unless you let them, unless you listen to them. You are beautiful and holy just the way you are.

That's what I want to say – the truth that God has given me to speak. I pray that one day I will have the courage to speak the truth, in all that I do, regardless of the consequences; that one day, when I meet God face-to-face, instead of asking why I didn't speak the truth I was given to speak, God will say, "Well done my good and faithful servant. Well done."

Chapter Seven

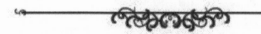

Absolution

I have been wondering how to end this book. I've given the previous chapters to some friends of mine to read and received positive feedback regarding its revelation of the struggles many of us face. I want to be able to tell you that things are getting better, that these struggles are being resolved, but I'm not sure they are. As one of my friends put it, "There's no happy ending here." And he's right, there's not— at least, not yet. There remains a major tension between the teachings of the Church and the truth that so many gay Catholics have discovered. Might this tension be productive?

From my psychology classes ages ago, I remember a professor saying, "Frustration brings about change." Indeed. Tension *does* bring about change. Struggle *is* part of the growing process. The apostle Paul says, "All creation is groaning."[xl] Right now, it seems to me, the Church is groaning, groaning on both sides of this issue. Is that a sign of hope? I think so. I think that it means there is hope, a hope rooted in a Church ultimately guided by the Holy Spirit as evidenced by the Church's continued existence, despite numerous comparable abuses by its leadership over the past 2000 years. There is no clearer evidence of the Holy Spirit at work in our Church than that – through it all, we have somehow

112

managed to survive and even grow. There *is* hope.

Having said that, I'm left wondering, where does that leave people like me? What's our next step? What should we do? That has been and will continue to be my prayer – *What should I do*? *What do you want me to do, Lord?* It was my prayer many years ago, and it led me to the priesthood. It is my prayer now, and it led me to this book. It will be my prayer in the future, leading me into places unknown. As I pray and wait for clarity, I realize, there *is* something I can do right now – and it's rooted in forgiveness.

***

In the Broadway Musical *BARE*, Peter and Jason are seniors in a Catholic boarding school preparing for their high school graduation. They have discovered their love for each other and, each in their own way, have tried to reconcile their homosexuality with what they've been taught by the Church. In the song "Cross," Jason seeks the advice of a priest during confession. After coming out to this priest, Jason, looking for acceptance and love, screams out: "What should I do?"

The response of the priest broke my heart: "Go keep it

quiet, I will hold your secret, you know that it's safe to confide...." [xli]He then tries to convince Jason to forget about it, to think about something else. When Jason insists that he can't just ignore it, the priest, who is now frustrated and angry, shouts back: "You know in your heart that the teaching is clear, Faith in the Father has led your soul here, Harrow the cross, let the Church be your spine, Don't question too much and you'll get along fine..."[xlii] Ugh.

These lyrics articulate so well the attitude and atmosphere with which the Church hierarchy surrounds gay Catholics. Harrow the cross, don't question too much, keep it a secret, keep it quiet and we'll get along fine. My heart sinks because I know this response all too well, it is the traditional response of the Church. Don't question too much. Don't push your agenda. Harrow the cross. Rather than feeling acceptance, love, and affirmation, gay Catholics are left feeling alone, isolated, silenced and shamed. I am sorry.

***

There are a few lines from the movie "Milk" that have stuck with me since the first time I saw it. In the scene when Harvey Milk is encouraging his supporters to come out to their families and friends, one of his supporters says, "There is such a thing as a right to privacy." To which Harvey Milk says, "Privacy's our enemy."[xliii] Silence is the enemy too. As much as I hate to admit this, silence by gay clergy might just be our biggest enemy when it comes to gay rights. If there is one thing we as a Church can learn from the scandal of 2002, it is that silence and secrets hurt us more than the truth.

Silence not only keeps people in the closet, it keeps fear alive. People fear what they don't understand. I've known good and faithful Catholics who have wonderful and generous hearts, and are yet adamantly opposed to homosexuality. They have all the right intentions, yet they will work tirelessly to oppose the civil rights of the LGBT community. It's sad, so incredibly sad. In their minds, they are keeping the faith, doing what they believe to be the good work of the Church. Bishops throughout the United States are spending millions to abolish, repeal or prevent same-sex marriage—Millions!—with the faithful, many of them, blindly supporting these efforts. We fear what we don't understand. I believe that getting to know someone who is gay can help us overcome our fears and misconceptions.

***

Later in the musical *BARE,* Jason dies of a drug overdose. In the production I saw, Jason is lying dead in the arms of a mourning Peter. The priest says to Peter, "At times like these, we will always ask ourselves if there was something more we could have done."

Peter's response is: "Do you ask yourself that Father?" [xliv]

Do you ask yourself that Father? I have to be honest with you, those words haunt me. They haunt me because I ask myself that question every time I read about another gay teenager committing suicide, or a group of teens bullying and beating up someone because they are gay, or the Church spending millions of dollars to stop gay marriage – is there more I could have done? Is there more I can do? Maybe we should all ask ourselves that question. *Is there more we could do?*

After Peter says, "Do you ask yourself that Father?" He sings the following lyrics:

PETER
"He went to you for guidance

You hid behind a screen

Knowing how much empathy might mean

Do you know how much he loved...?

Did you know how much he cared...?

Lost in the teaching was a...boy

So all alone and scared

Father, we were so in love!

And that's what I find so odd

Our love was pure and nothing else

Brought me closer to God"

PRIEST

"I'm sorry, Peter"

PETER

"I forgive you... Father"[xlv]

Wow...wow, "I forgive you Father." My prayer is often about forgiveness. "Please forgive me God for not doing more, for not speaking the truth you've given me to speak." And to all those teenagers who commit suicide, please forgive me, and to those who are persecuted because of their orientation, please forgive me, and to those who are hurt by bigotry and prejudice, please forgive me. Forgive me.

***

One day, I was meditating on forgiveness and asking for forgiveness in prayer, when the realization came to me that I must be willing to forgive the Church as well. I, like Peter, need to forgive the Church, the hierarchy, the anti-gay atmosphere which pervades our institutions. I need forgiveness, and I need to forgive.

A few years ago, I had the opportunity to go to Rome. While there, I spent time at the North American College, which is the college seminary responsible for educating American students. It was amazing, and in such a fantastic location, standing upon a hill overlooking the Vatican and the city of Rome. The view is incredible. It's not uncommon to visit the rooftop patio in the early evenings while the sun is setting over the city. I was there one evening, with a priest friend of mine who is also gay, discussing the Church's official position and reaffirmation to not ordain gay men to the priesthood. We were both acknowledging our anger and frustration with the Church hierarchy and our current Pope.

I turned to my friend and said, "Somehow, don't ask me how, we have to figure out a way to forgive the Church."

After a moment or two, my friend said, "That reminds me of a phrase I once heard about forgiveness. 'Forgiveness is letting go of the possibility of having a different or better past.'" Those words really caught my attention, so I took them with me to prayer and meditation for the next several months. You see, I know I need to forgive the Church, the Church hierarchy and all those whose words have hurt and oppressed others. The past is the past and there is nothing I or anyone can do to change it. What happened has happened. We have to let go of the possibility of having a different or better past. There is no possibility of ever changing the way the hierarchy responded to the priest pedophilia cases of the past decades, nor is there's any way of changing the anti-gay proclamations that have been issued by members of the hierarchy since. We can't go back and change what has already happened. Forgiveness is letting go of the possibility of having a different or better past.

The more I thought about that, the more it made sense to me that I needed to forgive the Church. But I also realized that letting go of the possibility of having a different or better past is not the same as letting go of the possibility of having a different or better future. We need to let go of the past and *work* towards a better future. We need to work towards a new Church, a more loving and inviting Church for all.

***

As I was meditating and praying upon just how desperately I want our Church to be more welcoming to gay and lesbian Catholics, I remembered a saying I heard a long time ago: "If you love the dream for the Church more than the Church itself, then you are the Church's enemy." There is an awful lot packed into that phrase. I wonder sometimes if I don't get dangerously close to becoming the Church's enemy on this issue – and I don't want to be the Church's enemy. As much as anyone, I love the Church that is, and I try to love it more than my dream for the Church. Some days I'm there, I think, but other days, not so much. Still, I *do* love the Church. I love the work we do, the love we show, our presence in the world. I steadfastly believe the world is a better place because of our Church. We, as a Church, do some amazing things – not always and not perfectly — but we, as a Church, are beautiful even in our imperfection. I love the Church. And I love my dream for the Church.

Some days, my dream for the Church and the Church itself are closer to the same thing than I might give the Church credit for, and some days, they are farther apart than I want to admit. And yet, I believe that by loving the Church that *is* more than the Church that *isn't*, I can be part of the process of change, of growth, of love. By loving the Church that is—the imperfect, big, beautiful people of God Church—more than the Church I want to be—a warm, inviting, loving, supportive and nourishing for all of God's people Church—I can help the Church to change and grow.

***

For more information about the author, please visit
www.fathergary.com

End Notes

Chapter 1 - Silent and Shamed

[i] "To preserve the mission of our schools, and to respect the faith of wider Catholic community, we expect all families who enroll students to live in accord with Catholic teaching. Parents living in open discord with Catholic teaching in areas of faith and morals unfortunately choose by their actions to disqualify their children from enrollment."
(2010, March 7). Catholic school rejects child because of lesbian parents. *ABC News*. Retrieved September 19, 2011 from
http://www.thedenverchannel.com/news/22769137/detail.html

[ii] Staff of the 8th Day Center for Justice. (January 2010). Statement on LGBT teen and young adult suicides. Retrieved September 19, 2011 from
http://www.newwaysministry.org/8th_Day_Center_Statement.html

[iii] (2011, June 26, 6 P.M.). CNN newsroom. *Transcripts*. Retrieved September 19, 2011 from
http://transcripts.cnn.com/TRANSCRIPTS/1106/26/cnr.02.html

[iv] Grillo, T. (2011, June 13). Church delays priests gay-friendly mass. *Boston Herald*. Retrieved September 19, 2011 from
http://www.bostonherald.com/news/regional/view.bg?articleid=1345040&format=comments#CommentsArea

[v] Mission and vision. *8th Day Center for Justice*. Retrieved September 19, 2011 from
http://www.8thdaycenter.org/?q=mission

Staff of the 8th Day Center for Justice. (January 2010). Statement on LGBT teen and young adult suicides. Retrieved September 19, 2011 from http://www.newwaysministry.org/8th_Day_Center_Statement.html

[vi] Ibid.

Chapter 2 – I Want to Be Out

[vii] Congregation for Catholic Education. (2005). Instruction concerning the criteria for the discernment of vocations with regard to persons with homosexual tendencies in view of their admission to the seminary and to holy orders. Vatican. Retrieved September 19, 2011 from http://www.vatican.va/roman_curia/congregations/ccatheduc/documents/rc_con_ccatheduc_doc_20051104_istruzione_en.html

[viii] John Jay College Research Team. (2011). The causes and context of sexual abuse of minors by Catholic priests in the United States, 1950-2010. Prepared for the U.S. Conference of Catholic Bishops. Retrieved September 19, 2011 from http://www.usccb.org/issues-and-action/child-and-youth-protection/upload/The-Causes-and-Context-of-Sexual-Abuse-of-Minors-by-Catholic-Priests-in-the-United-States-1950-2010.pdf

[ix] Martin, J., S.J. (2011, May 17). John Jay Report: On not blaming homosexual priests. *America magazine: The national Catholic weekly.* Retrieved September 19, 2011 from http://www.americamagazine.org/blog/entry.cfm?entry_id=4229

[x] Martin, J., S.J. (2000, November 4). The church and the homosexual priest. *America magazine: The national Catholic weekly.* Retrieved September 19, 2011 from

http://www.americamagazine.org/content/article.cfm?article
_id=2297

[xi] For a decent assessment of gay priests in the Catholic
Church visit http://www.religioustolerance.org/hom_rcc.htm

[xii] Glatz, C. (2008, December 3). Vatican opposes U.N. gay
support declaration. *National Catholic reporter.* Retrieved
September 19, 2011 from http://ncronline.org/node/2731

[xiii] Martin, J., S.J. (2010, May 25). USCCB letter on same-sex
marriage and ENDA. *America magazine: The national Catholic
weekly.* Retrieved September 19, 2011 from
http://www.americamagazine.org/blog/entry.cfm?entry_id=
2923

[xiv] 1 Corinthians 12:12

[xv] Jinks, D. (Producer), Cohen, J. (Producer), and Van Sant, G.
(Director). (2008). *Milk.* [Motion Picture]. United States:
Universal Pictures.

Chapter 4 – I Am Good at What I Do

[xvi] (2010, July 23). Catholic church lashes out at gay priests.
CBS News. Retrieved on September 19, 2011 from
http://www.cbsnews.com/stories/2010/07/23/world/main67
06927.shtml

[xvii] Cones, B. (2010, July 23). Gay priests giving gay priests a
bad name. *U.S. Catholics.* Retrieved September 19, 2011 from
http://www.uscatholic.org/blog/2010/07/gay-priests-giving-
gay-priests-bad-name

[xviii] McNaught, B. (2007). Keynote address. *Outward signs:
Lesbian/gay Catholics in a sacramental church.* [Symposium].
Minneapolis, MN.

xix Maguire, G. (2007). Address on Gay Parenting. *Outward signs: Lesbian/gay Catholics in a sacramental church.* [Symposium]. Minneapolis, MN.

xx Suicide Prevention Resource Center. (2008). Suicide risk and prevention for lesbian, gay, bisexual, and transgender youth. Newton, MA. Retrieved September 19, 2011 from http://www.sprc.org/library/SPRC_LGBT_Youth.pdf

xxi Karslake, D., (Producer and Director). (2007). For the Bible tells me so. [Motion Picture]. United States: Atticus Group and VisionQuest Productions.

Chapter 5 – Bash

xxii (2011). *Merriam-Webster Dictionary.* Retrieved September 19, 2011 from http://www.merriam-webster.com/dictionary/bash

xxiii Congregation for Catholic Education. (2005). Instruction concerning the criteria for the discernment of vocations with regard to persons with homosexual tendencies in view of their admission to the seminary and to holy orders. Vatican. Retrieved September 19, 2011 from http://www.vatican.va/roman_curia/congregations/ccatheduc/documents/rc_con_ccatheduc_doc_20051104_istruzione_en.html

xxiv Ibid.

xxv Ibid.

xxvi Ibid.

xxvii Ibid.

xxviii Simpson, B.J., OSJB. (2005, November 23). The self-destruction of the Roman Catholic church. *Christian gays.* Retrieved September 19, 2011 from http://christiangays.com/articles/bruce5.shtml

Chapter 6 – What I Want to Say

xxix King, M.L, Jr. (1963, April 16). Letter from Birmingham jail. Retrieved September 19, 2011 from http://www.africa.upenn.edu/Articles_Gen/Letter_Birmingham.html

xxx Prejean, H., CSJ. (2007). Address. *Outward signs: Lesbian/gay Catholics in a sacramental church.* [Symposium]. Minneapolis, MN.

xxxi More information about the campaign and links to videos can be found here http://www.itgetsbetter.org/

xxxii For more information about the Serenity Prayer visit http://en.wikipedia.org/wiki/Serenity_Prayer

xxxiii United States Conference of Catholic Bishops. (1976, November 11). To live in Christ Jesus: A pastoral reflection on the moral life. Washington, D.C.

xxxiv http://www.newwaysministry.org/

xxxv Melloy, K. (2010, May 12). Austrian cardinal: Church should respect long-term gay relationships. *EDGE Boston.* Retrieved September 19, 2011 from http://www.newwaysministry.org/05122010_Schonborn.html

xxxvi John Paul II, Pope. (1980, January 9). The nuptial meaning of the body. [General audience]. Vatican. Retrieved September 19, 2011 from

http://www.vatican.va/holy_father/john_paul_ii/audiences/catechesis_genesis/documents/hf_jp-ii_aud_19800109_en.html

xxxvii Paul, E. (2006). Did Galileo pray? *Ellis Paul Essentials.* [CD Recording]. Black Wolf Records.

xxxviii Ibid.

xxxix Ibid.

Chapter 7 – Absolution

xl Romans 8:22

xli Hartmere, J., Jr. and Intrabartolo, D. (2000). Cross. *BARE: A pop opera.* Theatrical Rights Worldwide. Retrieved September 19, 2011 from http://www.barethealbum.com/musical/

xlii Ibid.

xliii Jinks, D. (Producer), Cohen, J. (Producer), and Van Sant, G. (Director). (2008). *Milk.* [Motion Picture]. United States: Universal Pictures.

xliv Hartmere, J., Jr. and Intrabartolo, D. (2000). A Glooming Peace. *BARE: A pop opera.* Theatrical Rights Worldwide. Retrieved September 19, 2011 from http://www.barethealbum.com/musical/

xlv Hartmere, J., Jr. and Intrabartolo, D. (2000). Absolution. *BARE: A pop opera.* Theatrical Rights Worldwide. Retrieved September 19, 2011 from http://www.barethealbum.com/musical/